Against The Grain — Words For A Politically Incorrect Church

*Gospel Sermons For Sundays
After Pentecost (Last Third)
Cycle B*

Steven E. Albertin

CSS Publishing Company, Inc., Lima, Ohio

Copyright © 1999 by
CSS Publishing Company, Inc.
Lima, Ohio

Scripture quotations are from the *New Revised Standard Version of the Bible,* copyright
1989 by the Division of Christian Education of the National Council of the Churches of
Christ in the USA. Used by permission.

Library of Congress Cataloging-in-Publication Data

Albertin, Steven E., 1949 -
   Against the grain — words for a politically incorrect church : Gospel sermons for
Sundays after Pentecost (last third), Cycle B/ Steven E. Albertin.
      p.   cm.
   ISBN 0-7880-1503-6 (pbk. : alk. paper)
   1. Pentecost season Sermons. 2. Bible. N.T. Gospels Sermons. 3. Lutheran Church
Sermons. 4. Sermons, American. I. Title.
BV4300.5.A43   1999
252'.64—dc21

99-32757
CIP

This book is available in the following formats, listed by ISBN:
   0-7880-1503-6   Book
   0-7880-1504-4   Disk
   0-7880-1505-2   Sermon Prep

For more information about CSS Publishing Company resources, visit our website at
www.csspub.com.

PRINTED IN U.S.A.

To friend, colleague, and old classmate Marcus Lohrmann, whose friendship, commitment to the ministry, vision for the church, and understanding of the Gospel have sustained me in my ministry and my faith ... and whose encouragement has led to this collection of sermons.

Table Of Contents

Preface

We are what we are today because of the commitments we have consciously made and the contexts which have unconsciously shaped us. This interplay of personal commitment and context has also shaped this collection of sermons. In fact, these sermons ultimately cannot be understood and appreciated apart from these influences.

I grew up deeply shaped by the culture of the Lutheran Church, Missouri Synod. My father was an LCMS pastor for over forty years. I received a "classical education" in the LCMS "system" of education. I was shaped by the social turmoil of the '60s. I attended Concordia Seminary, St. Louis, during the heart of the controversy which tore apart the LCMS in the '70s. I was there when Concordia Seminary in Exile (Seminex) emerged from this conflict. During my life I have been part of three different Lutheran church bodies, and there still may be more to come.

I have also made several conscious commitments in my life which have shaped the direction of my ministry and personal life. I am committed to the gospel expressed in the theology of Lutheran Confessions. I am committed to the Law/Gospel hermeneutic, not only when it comes to understanding Scripture but life under God. I am committed to parish ministry. It is in local congregations that the church most engages culture and expresses its understanding of faith and mission. It is also in congregations that the church is most in danger of losing its identity and reason for being. In other words, the "cutting edge" of the church's life, the place where the most creative theologizing and ministry of the church must take place, is in the local congregation. That is why the longer I am in the ministry the more I am committed to the truth of that Reformation maxim, *semper reformans reformanda,* "always reforming the reformed." Therefore, the church, especially congregations and pastors, must always be self-critical and suspicious of their ministry. The danger of apostasy and compromise is always just around the next corner. The need to be continually reformed by God's Law and Gospel must remain central to the church's identity and mission — until Jesus comes again.

The sermons collected here reflect this context and these commitments. They reflect twenty-plus years of parish ministry in midwestern Lutheran congregations. They reflect the many theological conversations and debates I have had with fellow colleagues and pastors (especially Marcus Lohrmann), without which I fear my ministry too could have (and perhaps on occasion has) succumbed to apostasy and compromise.

It will be apparent to all who read these sermons that I am a product of the iconoclasm of the '60s and the church controversy that led to Seminex. As a result I have always been sympathetic to more sectarian and countercultural understandings of the church. I have always sensed that Christians have never really "fit" in this world. I have always been troubled by a church that is too enamored of "the big business of religion" and too hungry for the world's applause and approval. The church is first of all called to be faithful to the gospel, to be a sign of God's coming gracious kingdom in this world, and only secondarily to be a successful and competent institution in this world. This book is driven by the fear that the church has too often forgotten the former and succumbed to the latter.

Each of these sermons also reflects a very specific understanding of the gospel, an understanding described in Article 4 of both the Augsburg Confession and the Apology to the Augsburg Confession: justification by faith. I have failed to preach the gospel, and thereby a Christian sermon, if the gospel of justification by faith has not "happened" in these sermons. One of my most influential teachers, Ed Schroeder, taught me a simple little test by which to identify whether the gospel of justification by faith is "happening" in a sermon (or for that matter in any dimension of the church's ministry). He called it "the double dipstick test" (Ed was always great at coming up with clever and memorable teaching devices.)

8

1) Does this sermon *necessitate Christ*? In other words, is one saved only by a crucified and risen Christ or is something else necessary, e.g., the strength of my faith, my good works, my politically correct social stances, and so on? If so, then whatever it is that I am preaching is not the gospel! 2) When this message is proclaimed (i.e., the crucified and risen Christ has done it all for you!), then this message must by definition bring *comfort and consolation*. In other words, this message will always be good news! It can only be freely consented to. By definition it cannot coerce or threaten. It liberates. Therefore, whatever shape the response of the hearer takes, when someone consents to this good news, it is always a "get to." It can never be a "have to."

I hope that these sermons reflect this understanding of the gospel. I hope that they will be helpful to you as you seek not only to believe the gospel but also to proclaim it and live it in whatever context God has called you to serve. Most of all, I hope these sermons contribute to the ministry of congregations and the gospel that must be proclaimed in them. Without this happening, there may be a successful religious institution doing business down the street, but it is not the Christian Church.

Take Up
Your Ministry

Mark 9:38-50

Several years ago at my previous congregation I remember a discussion I had with the church council. It was very revealing of the kind of distorted vision of ministry that is very much afoot in the church these days.

I had a sudden change in my vacation plans and was going to have to be out of town for a Sunday that I had not planned on. I was having great difficulty finding another pastor to fill the pulpit. It was the summer. Many pastors are already on vacation and those who are available for pulpit supply were already booked. I suggested to the council that, if we continued to have a problem, we could call on one of several very capable lay people in the congregation, perhaps even one of them, to handle the preaching in my absence.

At first I think they thought I was joking, as a nervous laughter circulated around the room. But after a few moments, when it became obvious that I was serious and not joking, it got very quiet. The council members were visibly nervous. Everyone was avoiding eye contact with me for fear that I would ask one of them to do it. It was clear that none of them wanted to have any part of preaching. After all, preaching is for preachers and not lay people. That's my job, not theirs.

Eventually I was able to find a substitute, but this nervous crisis on the church council revealed a problem that afflicts Christian congregations everywhere. We have trouble understanding not only the nature of preaching but also the nature of the entire ministry of the church. I suspect that most think that ministry is only for the highly trained, for the seminary educated, called and ordained professional pastors. When we speak of being "called to *the* ministry," we usually think of the full-time professional ministry where people are salaried and paid by the church. Ministry is really not for the "lay" people, who by definition are only "amateurs." That is why they hire "professionals" — not only to do ministry on behalf of them but to do it better, because they are so highly skilled. If lay people do ministry, it must be "church" related work — like teaching Sunday school, singing in the choir, serving on the Council, volunteering to cut the grass or clean the sanctuary.

Most people have a difficult time seeing how they can possibly be "ministers" *out there* in the world of their everyday lives. If anything is to resemble ministry, then it had better resemble something which the "professional" minister gets paid to do. And that only seems to happen for lay people when we dress them up like pastors and they wear robes and help lead worship services. Or maybe when they "preach" or "witness" to some unbeliever. And since most lay people feel that they are not good at doing such things, since they do not have all the education and training of a pastor, they either feel guilty for not being better ministers or completely excuse themselves from having anything to do with the ministry of the church, except for supporting it financially, as they pay someone else to do it "for them." The ministry — preaching and teaching and counseling and talking about Jesus and raising money and running meetings — that's what the pastor is supposed to do for them. "After all, isn't that what we pay him for?"

During the last ten years the newly-formed Evangelical Lutheran Church in America has been wrestling with this problem of what is ministry and what isn't. Prior to the merger and the creation of this new denomination, several of its predecessor church bodies had very different understandings of what is "professional" ministry. One body recognized Christian day school teachers, deacons and deaconesses, ministers of music and education, along with ordained clergy as part of the one ministry of the church. Other bodies only recognized ordained, full-time clergy in a congregation. The recent Study on Mission attempted to resolve some of these differences. The recent controversy over "full communion" with the Episcopal Church is not only about the nature of the "historic episcopate" but is also about the nature of "ministry" in the church.

The question still has not been resolved, as revealed by the confusion that still exists in many congregations concerning who can preach and just who exactly is a minister and who is not. Is the ministry something reserved only for those who are rostered professionals, certified and approved by the church? Or is ministry more than that? Couldn't it be something given to all of God's people? And if so, just what is ministry and what is not? Is the ministry only something at which the laity can only hope to be good "amateurs" at best, especially when compared to the ordained "professionals" and "experts"? Today's scripture readings offer some help in answering these questions.

In today's Gospel, John, one of the innermost circle of Jesus' disciples, complains about a man who was casting out demons in the name of Jesus but was not one of Jesus' select group of twelve disciples. Today we might say that he was not on a clergy roster or a properly seminary-trained and certified professional church worker. Such breaking of official channels and institutional sanctions could not be tolerated. A similar incident is reported in today's First Lesson. Seventy elders were appointed to help Moses lead the Israelites in the wilderness. It had become too much for Moses to do by himself. But then we hear the complaints about two young men who were prophesying and were not among the seventy officially authorized elders.

Both Jesus and Moses respond in the same way and in a way which is remarkably unconcerned with following institutional sanctions. Both say that such unauthorized activity is okay! God doesn't always do his work though officially approved channels. Moses is elated that Eldad and Medad are prophesying and he wishes that more people in Israel were doing it. Jesus too is elated. This man who casts out demons in Jesus' name can't be all bad. In fact, what this man is doing is as important and as legitimate as what the select group of twelve were doing.

The message is clear. God will not be bound and his work will not be limited to "official channels." He is free to do what he wills where he wills. His Spirit blows freely and cannot be manipulated by our human connivances. Ministry, the work that God has given his people to do, can be carried out by a great variety of people. Ministry, the casting out of demons, the proclamation of God's Word, the giving of a cup of water to the parched and thirsty, is not something bequeathed to only a select few of God's people. Ministry, the mighty works done in the name of Jesus, cannot be controlled or limited by officialdom, church bureaucracies, congregational church councils, or even the pastor. Ministry is God's work. He gives it to whom he chooses. And the recipients of the responsibility may include those who we thought were least qualified.

What does this mean for you? The ministry is not just mine. It is not just something which is controlled by the officials of the church. This ministry is something which belongs to the whole people of God, all baptized Christians — and that means *you*! God has called you to be his servants in the world. He has given you time, talents, abilities, and money. The work you do on the job, in the community, in your homes, in the voting booth, that is God's work! By seeking to be faithful in your vocations, to do what is right and just and true, you are doing God's work. You are his servants and ministers.

But even more than this, it is through you out there in the world, outside the walls of this place, that the kingdom of Christ begins to take root in this world. As you give a cup of water to the thirsty, as you clothe the naked and feed the hungry, as you care for the welfare of a neighbor or a co-worker or even a rival, even at the expense of your own interests and well-being, as you forgive the wrongdoer and love your enemy, you begin to embody the sacrificial love of Christ to this world. You become the salt of the world, the seasoning of the earth. You begin to make a difference in this world, and the world begins to sit up and take notice.

I may be the pastor of this congregation, but you are the ministers of this congregation. My influence is confined to this small group of people. It is through your lives, through your influence, through your jobs, through your families, that this congregation most dramatically and most significantly impacts this community.

Not through me! I am only one person — but you are hundreds! It is through you that God ministers to and heals the world.

But I suspect that a lot of you see this as only a lot of idealistic talk, some pie-in-the-sky dreaming. Real life just isn't this way. So much of your work in life seems like just that — work. Your work easily becomes just a job, a drudgery, just a means to make a living. So much of it seems meaningless and purposeless and only does any good insofar as it puts food in your stomachs and roofs over your heads. To speak of work on the job, cleaning the diapers, disciplining the children, shuffling the papers in the office, putting patients on the bedpan, staring into a computer screen for hours as Christian ministry, as the work of God healing the world, seems utterly off the wall!

In a world where you must constantly deal with competitors and rivals, where advancement and promotion are all that seem to matter, where it seems that you had better look out for your own neck because no one else will, speaking of taking time out to give a cup of water to someone who is thirsty seems foolish, an inefficient use of time, even dangerous. In this world where everyone seems to be guarding his or her own turf, just like John in today's Gospel or Joshua in the First Lesson, you have got to look out for the upstarts who seem to pop up out of nowhere and threaten to infringe on that which you thought was yours and yours alone. After all, everyone for himself or herself — right?

Wrong! You may have thought you were on your own, slugging it out by yourself in this competitive world. You may even have wanted to be on your own without the thought of God complicating your plans. But you are not on your own! God won't let you alone. When you realize that you are accountable not just to yourself or those you want to impress but also to God, it makes you nervous. As you realize that the embarrassments and mistakes you may have wanted to keep out of sight cannot be hidden from God, that ought to make you nervous!

Or just when you thought you were most alone, when the demons and powers of the world have you most backed into a corner, when your lives seem most desperate and endangered, you ought to be looking for rescue!

And then surprisingly, in a way that you never anticipated, God comes to you through that unexpected visitor bearing that cup of water offering to quench your thirst, to salve your desperation. And likewise God comes to do his rescuing "in the name of Jesus" — in the waters of the font, in the eating and drinking of the table, in the tender touch, husky hug, and assuring words of an *unauthorized minister.* God comes to remind you that regardless of what the world might insinuate about you, regardless of how you might be accused by your own conscience or God's own holy presence, you are *nevertheless* his beloved children, his very own people, the apples of his eye — and yes, dare we say it? — his very own ministers, his chosen servants, his people sent to heal the world with a cup of water, with the love of God in Jesus Christ.

And there is absolutely *nothing* in this world that can take that promise away from you!

You can do it. Because you are salt. Because you are leaven. And because of who you are, you *can* make a difference in this world. You can be the ones who offer the cup of water to those who thirst. God is with you. God is in you. God is using you (*you* of all people!) to be his ministers.

Hard And
Soft Hearts

Mark 10:2-16

Probably one of the most frustrating responsibilities I have as a parish pastor is officiating at weddings. I would rather do a funeral than perform a wedding. It's not because I am filled with a great sense of morbidity. It's not that I delight in other people's suffering. Rather, it has to do with how receptive people are to ministry. At the time of death, people are much more receptive to facing the ultimate issues of life. They have a far greater sense of their need for the gospel. They have just experienced the limits of life and are primed to listen to the word of hope in Jesus Christ. However, at a wedding there are so many distractions that the last thing anyone wants to hear about is their need for the love of God in Jesus Christ. The focus is on the flowers, the dresses, the music, the reception, the party, the photographer. I think the time spent with the photographer is usually two or three times as long as the service. And you begin to wonder what is more important.

My frustration usually begins with the first premarital counseling session. There they sit like two lovebirds, usually holding hands and sneaking loving glances at one another.

"Why do you want to get married?"

Why, what a dumb question for the pastor to ask. They love each other! They love each other passionately. They can't stand to be separated from one another. They can't keep their hands off each other.

"Do you know what you are getting yourself into?"

What is wrong with this guy? They thought that he was in the business of marrying people. He should be glad that they are even

17

deciding to get married. Why, they could just go off and shack up together. In fact, they would not even be there if it wasn't for some parental pressure.

"If anyone knew what they were getting themselves into, they probably would never want to get married."

Now the pastor has really gone off the deep end. What is wrong with him? They are in love. They are enjoying the height of romantic bliss. They are anticipating one of the most happy days of their life and now he seems to want to spoil it all for them. It's almost as if he doesn't want them to get married.

Such an approach to premarital counseling may seem like I am trying to talk them out of getting married. It may seem like I am a spoilsport trying to ruin all their fun. It may seem like I am not even interested in marrying them. But that is not the case at all. I am deeply interested in helping them begin this new adventure in their lives. I want them to be happy. I want them to succeed in their marriage. It's just that marriage is such a wonderful gift from God. I what them to take full advantage of its benefits.

Our culture so distorts the true nature of marriage. And all the glitter and glamour associated with the wedding doesn't help the couple to realize what marriage is all about. Frankly, much of it is just a big distraction. It is sad to admit, but some of the most spectacular and expensive weddings I have participated in over the years of my ministry have resulted in marriages that were disasters.

Marriage is hard work. A friend of mine, who is a psychologist and counselor, once remarked to me that marriage is really "unnatural." Things that are natural come easily. But marriage is such hard work that it can't possibly be natural.

In the course of premarital counseling I often tell a couple: "You may think that you are getting married because you love one another. No, in fact it is quite the opposite. You are getting married in order to learn what it really means to love one another. Throughout your courtship you have probably been lying to one another. You have probably been patently dishonest with one another. When you date, you want to impress the other. You dress up in your best. You are on your best behavior. You make sure every hair is in place. You wear the cologne to make sure no one catches a whiff of any embarrassing odors. Tell me this is being honest with one another.

"Ah, but when you get married, the truth starts coming out. Then you can no longer so easily hide the truth. Then you discover what the other is really like because now he/she has promised to be with you until death parts you. Now you discover his/her stinky feet. Now you discover his/her short temper. Now you discover his/her disgusting personal habits. Now you get to see him/her early in the morning, sleep still blurring his/her eyes, sitting there on the toilet. Doesn't sound very romantic, does it? It really takes a lot of love to hang in there when your spouse is so unlovable. But it is then and only then that you begin to discover what marriage is really all about. Then and only then do you begin to discover what it really means to love."

Given those sorts of realities, I guess we should not be surprised that our society has become so littered with the rubble of broken marriages. According to the latest divorce statistics, half of all marriages end in divorce. The number of couples living together without the benefit of marriage increases daily. People have become so fearful of marriage that prenuptial agreements, unheard of a generation ago, are becoming much more common, especially among the middle and upper classes. In recent years the disastrous social consequences of being a single parent have been widely acknowledged. Yet, the mortality rate of marriage remains high. All of our families have been touched by the pain of divorce. We have come to accept it as a fact of modern life.

The moral stigma of divorce has all but disappeared. Our divorce laws reflect a society in which divorce is no longer the exception. The laws assume that divorce is "no-fault." Relationships change. People need to move on with their lives. Marriages can die. It's no one's fault. Don't make such a big deal out of divorce.

In today's "no-fault divorce" world Jesus' words in today's Gospel are troubling and unnerving. These are hard words. They not only challenge our society's ideas about divorce, they also raise some very troubling questions about our relationship to God. They remind us that none of our human relationships are trivial. They all ultimately reflect our relationship to God.

19

Today's Gospel begins with another confrontation between Jesus and those guardians of public morality, the Pharisees. We need to remind ourselves again and again that in the eyes of the common people the Pharisees were the good guys. They were the ones who took their religion seriously. They were first century Judaism's version of "Dr. Laura." They valued morality. They believed in character and integrity. They were serious about right and wrong. In the case of divorce, they had developed a complicated system of rules and regulations defining under what conditions divorce was right and wrong.

They came to test Jesus. They came to check him out on divorce. Jesus had created quite a controversy by hanging around with people of suspect moral character. He had even chosen a tax collector to be one of his disciples. He seemed a little too liberal, a little too permissive, when it came to the moral issues of right and wrong.

Jesus' response must have shocked them. Jesus absolutely prohibits divorce. Under no circumstances can divorce be justified before God. Quoting a portion of today's First Lesson from Genesis, Jesus shows that God's intention for marriage is that the union between man and woman be permanent. What God has joined together, no one else should separate.

In fact, it ultimately is a misunderstanding of this text to see it as Jesus providing moral advice on the issue of marriage and divorce. Jesus is no Dr. Laura, Ann Landers, or your friendly marriage counselor. Jesus wants to direct the Pharisees' attention to a deeper problem, their relationship to God. The Pharisees had staked their lives on the importance of knowing the difference between right and wrong. For them the question, "Is it lawful?" is the most important religious question you could ever ask. Your relationship to God is dependent upon being able to answer that question correctly. You couldn't do what was right if you didn't know what was right.

Jesus points out that they are missing the point. The problem of divorce reflects a far deeper problem. Moses permitted divorce under certain circumstances not because it was the right thing to do but only as a concession to human sin. Divorce can never be

20

Through The Eye Of A Needle

Mark 10:17-31

"It is easier for a camel to go through the eye of a needle than it is for a rich man to enter the kingdom of God."

It is sayings like this that shatter any notions we have of Jesus being simply another Mr. Nice Guy. These are tough words. They have been a flashpoint for controversy in the church for centuries. They have ignited heated debates about the role of money in the Christian life.

These tough words of Jesus have usually provoked two kinds of reactions. One interprets Jesus' words to mean that you had better give up your money. Money is at least a source of great temptation if not a tool of the devil himself. Therefore, if you want to be in the kingdom, give your money away and go off and join a monastery. The other perspective maintains that Jesus' words apply only to the rich. And since you're not rich, they don't apply to you.

Neither interpretation is very satisfactory. The first seems like an invitation to economic chaos. The second seems to be just too cavalier in dismissing Jesus' words.

Once, when I was discussing these very words with another clergy colleague of mine, he made a very revealing observation. Discussions and debates about who is rich and who is not miss the point. He argued that *the rich are those with enough money to be afraid of losing it.*

That puts Jesus' comments about riches and wealth into an entirely new context. Jesus' words urge us to look not at the amount of money we have but rather on the role money plays in our lives.

What is our *attitude* toward riches and wealth? If we have enough money so that we are afraid to lose it, then we are probably rich; then we are partners with this rich man; then it is probably easier for a camel to go through the eye of a needle than it is for *us* to enter the kingdom of God.

This passage is not going to be on the average Christian's list of his top ten favorite Bible passages. We don't like to talk about money, especially in church. We are probably more willing to talk about our sex lives than about how much money we make. Why is this so? Because more than anything else in our world, our money and how we use it reflects our deepest values and commitments. Look at how people spend their money and you will see their gods, what is their practical and everyday religion. After all, if we take Martin Luther seriously in what he says about the first commandment in his *Large Catechism*, then everyone has a god. There is no such thing as an atheist. Whatever we most love having and most fear losing is our functional god. Insofar as our use of money reflects these values and commitments, our use of money is a very "religious" issue.

No wonder Jesus talks so much about money in his sayings, teachings, and parables. There is no more "religious" subject in life. There is no other subject that gets so close to our hearts.

In our modern capitalist societies money is very important. Money is the measure of most, if not all, things. A good job with a good paycheck is the means to get all those good things which promise us the good life. That sounds like religion to me. You don't need to talk about God and heaven in order to talk about salvation.

In today's Gospel we meet a pious and godly man who also seems to be rich (if we compare this to the parallels in Matthew and Luke). He seems to be a guy who has got it all together, an ideal poster boy for *G.Q.* or *Christian Entrepreneur* (if there were such a magazine). He's young and handsome, and he not only drives a BMW but goes to church every week and doesn't miss a Promise Keepers' rally. He's probably got a cute perky wife, two children, and a nice house in the suburbs.

But all is not right. Something still bothers him. He knows deep down that these "gods" are leaving him empty. His monetary success still leaves him wanting. His anxiety and doubt are betrayed in the question he asks Jesus: "Good Teacher, what must I do to inherit eternal life?"

At first, he seems to be doing all the right things. He recognizes that his life is still empty, that money is not everything, and he seems to have come to the right place. He comes to Jesus to find an answer, to get his hungers filled, to become a disciple. It's hard to knock someone who's interested in Jesus.

That's why Jesus' reaction seems to be so strange. We thought Jesus was in the business of making disciples, but here he seems to brush the guy off. Why? This is not the way you become a disciple of Jesus. You don't volunteer to become a disciple of Jesus. You don't sign up for Christianity like signing up for the military or a membership at the local health club. No, Jesus takes the initiative. He's the one who does the recruiting.

Perhaps that is why Jesus is so put off by this man's attempt to butter him with his flattering "Good Teacher." Flattery will get you nowhere with Jesus. Likewise, the man's "What must I do?" question makes the wrong assumption. With such a question the man mistakenly assumes that he is capable of doing whatever it takes to impress Jesus and become one of his gang. His question betrays, on the one hand, his anxiety and, on the other hand, his arrogance. He thinks he can do it, if Jesus will only tell him how.

The man probably has good reason for his confidence. He has achieved all the symbols of success. According to Matthew and Luke he is rich, young, and a ruler. And most of all, he is pious. He takes his religion seriously. He is committed to God, or at least he thought so. He is good at keeping the commandments. He is a good person. He treats his neighbors well. The guy has an impeccable track record. Notice that Jesus doesn't challenge him. He doesn't accuse him of faking it a little here or there. He doesn't call him on the carpet for not being as good as he appears to be. This guy is good. Even Dr. Laura would be pleased with him.

But something is still not right. And Jesus knows it. This man has all the outward appearance of godliness. But his heart is still in the wrong place. And there is only one way Jesus can expose that heart. He tightens the screws. He goes after him with the First Commandment, that one commandment not even this rich, young, and pious ruler has been able to keep.

"Thou shalt have no other gods before me." But this man did have other gods at the center of his life: himself and his money. And there was only one way to show the man this truth he was avoiding. He would have to let go of his money and his desire to be in control.

"You lack one thing; go, sell what you have, and give to the poor, and you will have treasure in heaven; and come, follow me."

Despite his riches, his power, his youth, and his religious piety, he still lacked one thing. He did not trust God. And his inability to trust God, to keep the first commandment, and to let go of his idol was revealed when he unhappily walked away. He couldn't do it.

And Jesus sums it all up by saying, "It is harder for a camel to go through the eye of a needle than it is for a rich man to enter the kingdom of God."

The issue is not how much money is too much. The issue is not who is rich and who is not. Rather, the issue is this: Who do you trust? Do you trust yourself, your money, your good works, your popularity? Or do you trust the God who comes to you in Jesus and asks you to forsake all and follow him?

The disciples, who probably were impressed with this rich and powerful young man and would have liked to have one of such social and religious prestige in their group, were amazed. Shocked would be a better way to put it. If this man couldn't qualify to be a disciple, then who could? This demand that Jesus made of this man was ridiculous. It is impossible to keep.

Just think of it: what would happen if everyone would give away their money to the poor? It would be economic chaos. No economy could ever survive. No bank could stay open. No one could borrow money. No one could count on a fair day's wage for a fair day's work. Society would disintegrate. It would lead to death and destruction.

Jesus' demand is impossible to keep. If this is what it takes to be a disciple, if this is what it takes to be saved, then no one is saved. Then no one is worthy of being a disciple.

And that is precisely the point Jesus is trying to make — to the rich young ruler, to his disciples, and to us! As long as we ask, "What do I *have to* do?" as long as we think that our deeds or our money or our church attendance will count for something, as long as think we can do something to win God's approval, then we are stuck. Then we will never make it. Then we are like that camel stuck in the eye of the needle. Then we are like that rich young ruler who walked away from Jesus because it was *impossible* for him to give away his gods and trust Jesus.

When we come to this realization, Jesus has got us just where he wants us. When the disciples wondered if it would ever be possible for anyone to do what Jesus demanded, then Jesus had them just where he wanted them. What is impossible for us, for the rich young ruler, for the astonished disciples is possible for God! In fact, that is precisely the claim that Jesus was making for himself. That is what he came into this world to do: to accomplish the impossible, to do what only God can do, to pull us along with all the camels in the world through the eye of a needle.

No human being that has walked the face of the earth since Genesis 3 has been able to keep the first commandment. No human being since the fall into sin has been able to trust God and only God, above and before anything else. As impossible as it is for a camel to pass through the eye of a needle, so it is impossible for any of us to do what we are supposed to do to inherit eternal life. But what is impossible for us is possible with God! And that is exactly what God has done and is doing for us in Jesus Christ.

It may be impossible for us to trust God, but that doesn't stop God from trusting us. God sends Jesus into this world to forgive and embrace chronic idolaters like you and me and the rich young ruler and the astonished disciples. In Jesus Christ we at last meet a God we can totally trust. When we come to his table to eat and to drink, there are no limits on the portions. There is no food rationing here. There is no limited supply of God's love. There is no sin too great. There is no doubt too deep. There is no crime so great that God cannot forgive. Dare we say it: there is no needle too small with an eye too tiny through which the grace of God cannot pull us.

When water is poured and God's promise is spoken at the baptismal font, there is no statute of limitations. This is a promise that lasts forever. It will never wear out. It will never need to be repeated, as if somehow it didn't work the first time.

And when we let God love us like this, life changes. It can no longer be business as usual. And we begin to find ourselves doing wonderful and marvelous things, even miracles. Suddenly camels pass though the eyes of needles. And people who live in a world where money means everything are suddenly able to do things with money that seem strange to the rest of the world.

We are shortly in our worship service going to engage in one of the most radical and countercultural actions of the liturgy. We are going to be giving an offering to the church and God. To the outsider it looks very ordinary. It looks like just another fundraising activity in a money-dominated culture. Clubs ask you to pay your dues. Churches ask you to make your contributions. Just like the coffee shop down the street, churches expect you to pay for services rendered.

It may look that way to the outside, but that is not what it is at all. That is why we insist on calling it an offering and not dues or obligations or a collection. In Jesus Christ God has brought us into a new world called the kingdom of God. In this world there are no limits. We live trusting that, when it comes to God's love and his promises, there is no scarcity. There is only abundance. And so we do what seems absurd to the rest of our world. We give our money away — freely, generously, joyfully. And no one is twisting our arms. No one is forcing us. We have no expectation of getting anything in return. We give ourselves away in the form of our money, not because we *have to* but because we *want to*.

In a world where there never seems to be enough money to go around, in a world where we are always haunted by the specter of scarcity, in a world where time is money and money is power, in a world where a solid return on your investment is the most sacred value of all, in a world where no camel is ever going to pass through the eye of a needle and where no one in their right mind is ever going to give money away freely and willingly to others expecting nothing in return, in a world filled with such impossibilities, all things are possible with God in Jesus Christ. And those impossibilities are not only possible, they happen. They are reality here in this place today as Jesus blesses us with his grace.

"What's In It For Me?"

Mark 10:35-45

One of the most dominating characteristics of our modern American culture is our worship of the free market. We live in a society where the free market reigns supreme. The free market determines which companies will profit and which will go out of business. The free market determines which political party will win the election. The free market determines which products will sell. The free market determines which ideas will triumph.

The free market is the people. The marketplace is where people shop for the best. In the marketplace the people are always asking the question, "What's in it for me?" In the marketplace the needs of the consumer reign supreme. In order for me to buy your widget, in order for me to vote for your candidate, in order for me to believe your idea, you must show me how it meets my needs. It must deliver on what it promises to give me. If it fails to do so, as a member of the marketplace I am free to choose another product that promises to better meet my needs.

Even the churches have not escaped the power of the marketplace. This is most evident in the current practice of "church shopping." This is a free market. People are free to shop for the religion, for the church, that best meets their needs. The churches that are best able to serve the needs of the consumer grow and thrive. The churches that fail to meet the needs of the consumer shrink and die.

Some have looked to the empty, established state churches of Europe as classic examples of what happens when you don't have a free market. In many of those countries, there is one official state religion. It is given all sorts of privileges by the state. It gets to operate a religious monopoly. It is supported by state taxes. It is a kind of religious socialism. But, as we have seen happen to many socialistic experiments in the last generation, official state protection breeds laziness, inefficiency, incompetence. In these state church societies, churches have had their survival guaranteed. Therefore, they don't have to be sensitive to the needs of the consumers. They can afford to become lazy and inefficient. The only choice that the consumers have is to stop going to church. They look elsewhere to get their religious needs filled. By way of contrast, in this country churches are relatively well attended because here no one has a religious monopoly. They all need to compete. They all need to be "lean and mean." It is survival of the fittest. Those who are able to meet the needs of the consumer succeed. Those who do not fail.

In this free market religious economy where "church shopping" reigns supreme, the needs of the consumer are most important. The consumer will always ask, "What's in it for me?" In other words, how can you meet my religious needs? What can you do to save my marriage, save my family, save my job, save my sanity, save my sense of well-being, save my soul? If you can't do this for me, I'll just go down the aisle of the religious supermarket and shop for a better product.

"What's in it for me?" That also seems to be the concern behind the questions James and John have for Jesus in today's Gospel. "Teacher, we want you to do for us whatever we ask of you." In other words, James and John want Jesus to satisfy their needs. They want Jesus to give them whatever they want.

They knew that Jesus was something special. They suspected that he was the Messiah. They were looking forward to finally setting up his kingdom. They were looking forward to Jesus finally solving their problems. And, of course, like any normal human being, they wanted to get their piece of the pie.

"Grant us to sit, one at your right hand and one at your left, in your glory." They wanted special places of privilege in Jesus' kingdom. How about making one of them Secretary of State and the other Secretary of the Treasury?

Jesus' response is not what James and John anticipated. "You do not know what you are asking." Are you sure you want to have such places of privilege and honor in my kingdom? Are you sure you want me to give you what you really need? Do you really want to be a big shot in my kingdom? "Are you able to drink the cup that I drink, or be baptized with the baptism that I am baptized with?"

What a strange answer. What does Jesus mean with this talk of drinking a cup and being baptized? "To drink the cup" is a colloquialism, a manner of speaking, an idiom that was occasionally used in the Old Testament to refer to one accepting one's inevitable destiny. To drink one's cup was to accept one's fate. To drink one's cup was to accept what was most inevitable in anyone's fate: death. In other words, to drink the cup would be to accept the same inevitable fate that Jesus was about to accept: his suffering and death. Jesus would later use this same phrase in the Garden of Gethsemane when he struggled to accept his imminent death and prayed that his Father not ask him "to drink the cup of suffering."

"Baptism" is also used by Jesus in a way that is very different from the way we use it today. In this church when we speak of a baptism, we probably all think of a small baby being brought to the baptismal font and being gently washed (or at least sprinkled) with water. These baptisms seem to be such pleasant and happy events. The little child is washed clean. The dirt of sin is washed away.

But the image of "baptism" in the ancient world was much more dramatic than this. Being baptized is not like washing your hands or taking a bath. Being baptized is not some pleasant and useful way to get clean. On the contrary, being baptized was to be overwhelmed with water, to be submerged, drowned, killed in a flood. In other words, when Jesus spoke of his coming baptism, he was referring to his coming death on the cross. He was soon to be overwhelmed, drowned in the waters of death.

Do you disciples know what you are asking? Places of glory and honor in Jesus' kingdom means drinking of the cup of suffering. Places of honor in Jesus' kingdom means baptism in the waters of death.

"What's in it for me?" James and John thought it would mean celebrity and fame and power. And Jesus tells them it will mean suffering and death.

Did they get it? Did they understand what Jesus was talking about? They thought they did. "We are able." They are sure that they will be able to drink the cup and be baptized with Jesus' baptism. They almost seem eager to do it. But as we see by their subsequent behavior, they still didn't have any idea of what Jesus was talking about.

When later they are in the Garden of Gethsemane and Jesus knows he is facing imminent trouble and prays that this "cup" be removed from him, where are these disciples? Where are these friends and supporters of Jesus who are so willing to take places of honor in his kingdom? Asleep. And when Jesus is finally arrested a few moments later, where are these disciples who were so willing to drink the cup and be baptized with Jesus' baptism? They flee into the night. And where are these disciples when Jesus is finally drinking the cup of his destiny on the cross and being overwhelmed in the baptism of his crucifixion? They are nowhere to be found.

"Yes, Lord, we are able! Sure, we are ready to take our places of glory! Yeah, we are ready to drink the cup! Of course, give us your baptism!"

Oh, if they only knew for what they were asking.

The other ten disciples can't help but overhear this conversation. They too wonder, "What's in it for me?" They too want their piece of the action. They too want their places of glory. They too want the best seats in the house. And they are angry with James and John for trying to cut in line in front of them.

Jesus has obviously had it with such open displays of shameless ambition. These eager disciples obviously don't get it.

"So you guys want places of glory? So you people want places of privilege in my kingdom? So, you want to know, 'What's in it for me?' Well, let me tell you."

Jesus then describes what it means to have places of honor and privilege in his kingdom. And what he tells them must have totally surprised and shocked them.

"So, you want to sit at my right and left hand? So you want to be big shots? Well, in my kingdom it's not like the rest of the world. Being a big shot in my kingdom doesn't mean being king of the mountain. It doesn't mean being CEO or Chairman of the Board. It doesn't mean getting to tell others what to do. It doesn't mean having an unlimited expense account to live high on the hog. It doesn't mean having everyone wait on your needs or having everyone kiss your feet. No, it is not so among you; but whoever wishes to become great among you must be your servant, and whoever wishes to be first among you must be slave of all. In my kingdom you get to serve, to sacrifice, to give yourself away for others. In my kingdom you get to drink the cup. You get to be baptized with my baptism. You get to die!"

"What's in it for me?" If this is what is in it for James and John and the other ten disciples and for you and me, then why would anyone ever want to be a disciple of Jesus? Who in their right mind would ever want to be a part of this gang? Who would ever want to become a member of this congregation? Who would ever want to be a Christian? No one in their right mind would ever want to have any part of this kind of life. We want to have a church, a God, a messiah that serve our needs and help us get to the front of the line.

What's in this for me? It doesn't look like much. Who wants to serve and sacrifice and give themselves away? Who wants to die? Not many people that I know.

The "What's in it for me?" question that drives the modern religious marketplace is very revealing. It reveals that at the heart of every religious quest for "salvation" is the "self" that wants to survive. We want to stay in control. Like the disciples, we are sure that we can do it.

"Pastor, just tell me what I have to do. Just tell me what I have to believe. I know I can do it. I know I am able."

Are we able to drink the cup? Are we able to be baptized with Jesus' baptism? Are we able let go of ourselves and our preoccupation with trying to stay in control? Ever since Genesis 3 every human being that has ever walked the earth has resisted drinking the cup or being baptized with the baptism. We can't trust God.

We can't let go. We have to run our lives the way we want. We can't help but ask, "What's in it for me?"

Every human being that has ever walked the face of the earth has resisted making such self-sacrifice. Except for one. Except for the one who said, "I came not to be served but to serve and give my life as a ransom for many." Watch him. He lives his life as a servant. He gives his life away in the service of others. "What's in it for me?" seems to be the furthest thing from his mind. Instead he lives his life filled with a strange sense of confidence. He knows who he is. He knows God is his Father. He trusts his future. There is no reason to hold on to his life, as if somehow he must save himself. Instead he gives himself away, even all the way to death on a cross.

And he was no fool who believed in an empty dream. He dared to trust the love of his Father. And he dared to invite others to trust the same. And when he was raised from the dead three days later, the creator of heaven and earth, the one whom Jesus dared to call his Father, announced to the world that Jesus was not mistaken. His faith was not in vain. Jesus was right.

At the end of today's Gospel Jesus calls himself a "ransom." You pay a ransom in order to set someone else free. You pay the price to get someone else out of bondage. Jesus insists that his coming death will be his ransom, his sacrifice for us. He changes places with us. As Martin Luther once described it, Jesus was the "sweet swap" for us. In his death and resurrection he exchanged our fate for his fate. He exchanged our sin for his righteousness. He exchanged his life for our death. He became a curse for us so that we might be free — free from that sinful obsession always to serve ourselves, from that sinful obsession always to ask, "What's in it for me?"

James and John and the other ten and even you and I are unable on our own to let go of our drive for survival. We can't stop asking, "What's in it for me?" But Jesus dies for us. And because he dies for us, we can have that place of honor and privilege we so desperately want.

When we come to his table to eat and drink, he is granting us that place of honor at his right and at his left hand. When water was poured over us in the name of Jesus, we were granted that place of glory at the table of God's great banquet. When Jesus became the "ransom," when he suffered, died, and was raised again, he did it "for us." He did it so that we might sit at his right and his left hand.

And because of what he did, we are rich. We have places of honor at his table. We are the beloved sons and daughters of God. And therefore, we can begin to give ourselves away. Therefore, we can begin to serve and sacrifice. Therefore, we can afford to let go, to die, to drink the cup and be baptized with the baptism.

In the drama of our liturgy we get to act out this new kind of life that is already ours in Christ. We get to drink the cup and be baptized with the baptism and let go of ourselves and be a servant and die.

We begin the service by confessing our sins. If there is anything that is like dying a little, it is admitting that we are wrong. Yet, we get to confess our sins. We get to die a little, because we already have been forgiven. We already have the seats of privilege in the kingdom.

We give away our money in an offering. Can you imagine it — giving away the most important source of power and prestige in our society and expecting to get nothing in return, giving away our money for the sake of others, for the sake of the mission of the church?

At the end of the service we are reminded, "Go in peace. Serve the Lord." Serve the Lord! Give ourselves away for the sake of God, not for what we can get out of it, but for the sake of God! "What's in it for me?" is no longer an issue.

Can you imagine forgiving someone who has wronged you? They have kicked you in the shins. They have hurt you. You have every right in the world to demand some justice. You deserve some sort of payback. But to forgive is to forego your legitimate right for justice. To forgive is to give up your right to get even. To forgive is to die a little. To forgive is not to demand your "pound of flesh." To forgive is to drink the cup. To forgive is to be baptized with Jesus' baptism.

It is so difficult for congregations in this world not to be concerned about their own survival. It is so difficult to be a servant, to give the life of the congregation away for the sake of the world, when there are bills to pay and salaries to make. One of our local pastors once shared with me a story of an experience he had when he was on internship. His internship supervisor was an old crusty, no-nonsense kind of pastor. Together they served in the inner city. Each month at the church council meeting, the members of the council would complain about the children in the neighborhood who would litter the parking lot, damage the flowers, and break the church windows. This complaining went on month after month. Finally in frustration the old pastor said to his council, "Well, are we going to pass a motion to kill the damn kids?" In his frustration and with this expletive the pastor wanted to remind his council why they were there in that neighborhood in the first place. They were there to serve, to give their lives away as a ransom for many — even for those children in the neighborhood.

"What's in it for me?" What's in it for you and me as we sit at our places of honor in the kingdom? The privilege, the honor, the opportunity to give ourselves away, to serve, to die for the sake of the world. That is the only way to live in Jesus' kingdom.

Do You See What I See?

Mark 10:46-52

There is a gentle and quaint Christmas carol in which the shepherds of Bethlehem point out to everyone they meet on their way the marvel they have seen in the manger. "Do you see what I see?" they ask all those gathered in Bethlehem. According to this Christmas carol, this birth, which had taken place under the most plain and ordinary of circumstances, would surely have been overlooked were it not for those shepherds who called it to everyone's attention by exclaiming, "Do you see what I see?"

In my church secretary's office there hangs a modernistic picture composed of a maze of colors and shapes. I know these sophisticated, modern, and abstract pictures are supposed to contain some profound artistic or philosophical message, but I have never been able to figure it out. It just looks like a jumbled mass of confusion. If there is a message there, I am blind to it.

One day while I was standing in the office, waiting for the copier to warm up, one of the congregation's kindergarten-age boys, Adam, stood beside me and said, "Do you see what I see?"

"Do you see something in that picture? I sure don't."

Adam looked at me with glee in his eye, "Pastor, can't you see him? It's Jesus hanging on the cross."

I stared as hard as I could, until my eyes actually hurt from staring. I wanted to believe Adam and that there actually was the image of Jesus hanging on the cross hidden somewhere in that mass of color and shapes, but I couldn't see Jesus anywhere. "Adam, I'm sorry but I must be blind. You will have to help me see."

41

Directing his finger to a mass of color in the center of the picture, Adam said, "There, Pastor. Do you see what I see? There is Jesus, his face, his arms outstretched on the cross."

And then, like an epiphany, the image began to appear. Yes, there hidden somehow "behind" the colors and the shapes was the barely visible image of Jesus, hanging with arms outstretched on the cross. "It's amazing, Adam. You have helped one blind pastor to see Jesus. Yes, I can see what you see, Adam."

A similar epiphany happens in today's Gospel. There we meet Bartimaeus, a blind man, son of Timaeus of Jericho, who comes to us with the same question asked by the shepherds in that quaint Christmas carol, who comes to us with the same question asked me by Adam: "Do you see what I see?"

Ironically, it is from those places and people we least expect it that God often makes his most stunning revelations to us. God uses shepherds, kindergarten boys, blind Bartimaeus, a crucified carpenter's son from an out-of-the-way place and an out-of-the-way time, a sip of wine and bit of bread, the pouring of water, the caring hands and firm embraces of ordinary Christians, to help us to see what is ordinarily hidden. God uses them to help us see the most important thing in the world: his love for us in Jesus.

But there is a problem in all of this. We live in a world where no one seems to be able to make any firm and sure claims about anything. In the last generation our society has come under the influence of a way of thinking called "post-modernism." In this world there are nothing but competing interests and points of view. There is no consensus about anything. The only absolute is that nothing is absolute. Everyone has a point-of-view, an ax to grind, a bias to promote.

For example, Indiana University and Purdue fans may watch the same basketball game but have two very different interpretations of what went on. Today we are continually reminded that affluent suburban whites and poor urban minorities see this society and its opportunities in two very different ways. The same could be said for the residents of the developed countries of the first world and the residents of the undeveloped countries of the third world. A divorced mother of three is obviously going to look at marriage much differently than the couple who is celebrating their fiftieth wedding anniversary. With the way Republicans and Democrats view the political issues of our society, one wonders whether they live in the same country. The bottom line in such a world of relativism, pluralism, and diversity is that truth and value are ultimately determined by those with the most bucks, the most guns, or the most votes. Whoever is in power controls the truth. Our world is a world in which we live and die by the polls. Who needs God? We've got Gallup!

In this kind of world the words of Bartimaeus seem all the more incredible. "Do you see what I see? Do you see that Jesus is the Messiah — and he can heal me — and you?" How can Bartimaeus claim to see anything? He has no credibility.

First of all, Bartimaeus was just another one of the "multitude" in the Gospel of Mark. In Mark the "multitude" is the *ochloi*, the great unwashed masses, those anonymous faces who always seem to exist on the fringes of every society. The *ochloi* are those who sit in the bleachers, if they can afford seats at all. The *ochloi* shop at Goodwill or Big Lots or at the clearance sale at K-Mart. The *ochloi* have no college degrees, drive used cars, and live from paycheck to paycheck. The *ochloi* don't bother to vote any more because voting just means exchanging one crooked politician for another. In other words, Bartimaeus doesn't matter. His opinions don't count. He's just one of the crowd.

On top of that, Bartimaeus is a beggar. This guy is a welfare slouch. He doesn't even hold down a job. He doesn't pay taxes. He just lives off the generosity of others. He doesn't have much spending power. Market researchers don't care what beggars think when they are developing their next product. They only care about those with the spendable income. And that doesn't include beggars like Bartimaeus. He doesn't count.

And most of all, Bartimaeus is blind. He can't see. He can't tell night from day. He can't tell ugly from pretty. He can't read or write. He stumbles around his bleak world swinging his stick in front of him, hoping he doesn't walk out into a busy street or step off a cliff. Who cares what Bartimaeus can see or thinks about anything? In our visual world where appearances and looks mean everything, who wants to hear from someone who can't see what is around the next corner?

No wonder all those in the crowd rebuked and ridiculed Bartimaeus when he said, "Do you see what I see?" Bartimaeus claimed to see what no one else saw: the Messiah. Bartimaeus believed that this Jesus of Nazareth, this wandering preacher and ordinary son of Joseph, the carpenter from that little hick town up north, Nazareth, was "the Son of David." That was no ordinary title. To call Jesus "the Son of David" was Bartimaeus' way of claiming that Jesus was, in fact, the long-awaited Messiah, the descendant of King David, the king of Israel, who would finally fulfill all the hopes and dreams of God's people.

Bartimaeus speaks the same words to us: "Do you see what I see?" Bartimaeus sees Jesus as the ultimate answer to all human striving. Bartimaeus sees Jesus as the final and absolute truth in a world where no one seems to have the nerve to make a claim for the truth of anything. Bartimaeus believes that Jesus has the power to heal his ailment in a world where the only ones who can make such claims are those with the bucks, the guns, and the votes. And Bartimaeus has none of these. Yet, he still believes. And he invites us to believe the same today: "Do you see what I see? Do you believe what I believe?"

It would be tempting to see Bartimaeus as a heroic example of faith. He was unwilling to give up his conviction that Jesus was the Messiah. He had courage. He hung in there even when others discouraged him. He could be seen as a clinical example of the healing powers of faith. See, if you believe hard enough, persistently enough, sufficiently enough, strongly enough, then you will not be disappointed, then you will be healed, then you will be saved.

But that is not what is going on in this story. Yes, Bartimaeus is a key figure, but he is key only because of his relationship to Jesus. And Bartimaeus is always *responding to* Jesus, who is always taking the *initiative*. Bartimaeus is moved when he hears the word that Jesus is near. It is in response to what he has heard about Jesus that Bartimaeus dares to come to his outrageous conclusion: that Jesus is the Messiah and that he can heal Bartimaeus. Bartimaeus' faith is not in himself, his own courage, and his own

44

ability to hope even in the face of hopelessness. No, Bartimaeus' faith is not in himself at all but in Jesus. Jesus is the one who encourages and nurtures this faith. And Jesus is the one who finally fulfills Bartimaeus' faith by healing him of his blindness.

It was not that Bartimaeus' faith was so great. No, rather it was the one in whom Bartimaeus believed who was so great.

Bartimaeus' faith in Jesus was not in vain. He was not disappointed. Jesus agreed with what Bartimaeus saw in him. And to prove it, he healed him.

What was it that Bartimaeus saw in Jesus? What is Bartimaeus asking us to see in Jesus? Not only that he is the long-awaited Davidic Messiah, not only that he had the power to undo Bartimaeus' predicament, but that Jesus cared *about him*! In a world where Bartimaeus had nothing going for him, where it seemed that only the rich and powerful were important, where no one could be trusted, where he had every reason *not to believe* that he was important, in spite of all this evidence to the contrary, Bartimaeus "saw" in Jesus the love of God *for him*. And that faith was not in vain. What Bartimaeus "saw" in Jesus by faith and not by sight, Jesus finally granted to him by sight and not just by faith. Bartimaeus was healed of his blindness.

Bartimaeus lives among us now. Bartimaeus is here now asking us the same question: "Do you see what I see? Do you see that God *cares for you* even though you may be on the fringes of earthly power, anonymous numbers in the *ochloi*? Do you see that in this world where everyone has a spin, where nothing is as it seems, where everyone has an agenda, where everyone is 'on the make,' that here is someone you can trust — Jesus?"

"Do you see what I see?" asks Bartimaeus. "Jesus is here, alive, now, in this place, among us. In a world where the truth is reinvented every day by whomever has the power, here we gather to confess a creed that has been handed down for almost 2,000 years unchanged, untainted, unabridged by the power of guns, bucks, and votes."

"Do you see what I see?" asks Bartimaeus. "In a world where there are always strings attached, where there is no such thing as something for nothing, where no one gives you anything without an expectation of getting something in return, here we receive the love and kindness of others, of God, with no questions asked."

"Do you see what I see?" asks Bartimaeus. "In a world of situational ethics, where 'if it feels good, do it,' where morality is determined by majority vote, where goodness and righteousness are good and right if they are good *for me*, here is a place where right and wrong are not measured by the latest opinion poll."

"Don't you see what I see?" asks Bartimaeus. "In a world where everyone else is trying to keep score, working to get one up on you and always arguing that they are right, as if their lives depended upon it, here things are different. Here you can afford to admit your mistakes, confess your sins, and acknowledge that you are wrong, because here you know that your life does not depend on being right but on the righteousness of Jesus."

"Do you see what I see?" asks Bartimaeus. "Here you can actually pray to someone, to God. Here prayer is not just crossing your fingers and hoping that things will turn out all right. Here prayer is not the last act of desperation but the first line of attack. Here prayer is not just something you do because it makes you feel good but is something that actually changes things. Here prayers are answered. Here miracles happen. Here the blind see. Here what previously was hidden is now revealed."

Let me tell you the story of Hilda. For over fifteen years in Fort Wayne I served as a chaplain in a local nursing home. Over the course of fifteen years you see a lot of lives go past you. One such life was Hilda.

Hilda loved to come to my Thursday morning worship services. She was an old feisty German on the outside, but on the inside she was tender and soft and loved Jesus. Hilda suffered badly from diabetes. She was losing her eyesight. She was almost totally blind. She was confined to a wheelchair because of the poor circulation in her legs. Every few months she would have less of her legs because of another amputation she had to endure.

But Hilda was never discouraged. She never missed a Thursday service because she loved to sing the songs, listen to Scripture, hear a message, but most of all to pray. Every week I would take special prayer petitions and requests from the residents gathered there. It never failed. Hilda always requested a prayer for the healing and the restoration of her eyesight. As her health deteriorated, I expected her to become more realistic and modify those prayers for healing. Maybe she would someday accept the inevitable. But Hilda kept on praying. She always said, "If God raised Jesus from the dead, then God can heal me, then God will make me see."

One Thursday I noticed that Hilda was absent. My fears were realized. Hilda had passed away the previous week. But before I could utter a prayer for Hilda's family and friends, now mourning her death, one of the regular residents interrupted me and said, "Don't you think we should offer God a prayer of thanksgiving?"

"Oh, sure," I thought. "We need to thank God for giving us Hilda to know as a friend and sister in the faith."

"Oh, yes, Pastor, we can pray for that. But how about thanking God for answering Hilda's prayer?"

"Oh certainly," I said. "We need to thank God for answering Hilda's prayer and taking her to heaven."

The resident was now getting impatient with me. "But, Pastor, not that prayer! Let's thank God for finally healing Hilda and giving her back her eyesight."

"But Hilda wasn't healed. She died!" I insisted with a firm sense of objectivity.

"But, Pastor, Jesus took Hilda home. And Jesus heals all his friends. That's why I know that Hilda is finally getting to see."

And I thought to myself, Hilda had been blind, but she saw clearly, more clearly that the rest of us. Like blind Bartimaeus before her, she saw Jesus and trusted him. During all those weeks and months she came to weekly worship that was what she wanted me to see. But I was blind to it. It was as if Hilda was telling me; it was as if she was telling all of us: "Do you see what I see?"

Hilda may have been blind. Bartimaeus may have been blind. But because they saw Jesus for what he truly was, they could really see. And what they saw by faith was eventually granted to their sight. Bartimaeus was healed. And so was Hilda. That same Jesus is here, now, among us, in this place, to help us see what Bartimaeus and Hilda saw, the only thing that really matters in this whole wide world: Jesus!

Baptism And Self-Esteem

Mark 12:28-34

Every once in awhile I am surprised by a film which offers a message that I never expected. When I checked out *Brubaker*, an old Robert Redford film from the late '70s, from my local video store I expected some romantic adventure from one of Hollywood's biggest stars. That's not at all what I got. Instead I saw a wonderful and thought-provoking portrayal of human nature. *Brubaker* turned out to be a spellbinding film about the futile attempt of an enlightened prison warden to reform a hopelessly corrupt prison. Brubaker was the name of the warden, played by Robert Redford, who had dramatic success in reforming a prison, but then was run out of his job by a prison board which didn't want the system to change.

Brubaker was enormously successful in reforming his prison for several reasons. The most startling and controversial aspect of his reform program was the way he sought to treat his prisoners. Other wardens had only concentrated on controlling the behavior of the prisoners. The prisoners were often demeaned, humiliated, and treated as if they were nothing more than animals. Brubaker treated his prisoners much differently. He insisted that if they were treated like animals, they would behave like animals. To behave like respectable and responsible human beings, they needed to have what every respectable and responsible human being must have: self-esteem. Brubaker gave it to them and it transformed the prison.

There is one scene which especially illustrates how Brubaker used the prisoners' need for self-esteem to reform the prison. As the new warden, one of the first things he insists on creating is a council made up of prisoners which would govern the affairs of the prison. The election has just been completed and the council is meeting for the first time outside the warden's office. It is a motley group of characters. They all sit in silence around the table waiting for something to happen. The time drags on. The silence, so it seems, lasts for an eternity. There are only empty stares. No one says a word.

In walks Brubaker with his nose buried in some papers. He seems unconcerned with the meeting. Suddenly he stops and asks, "What are you guys waiting for? You won the election. This is your council."

There is still only silence. A look of nervousness, almost fear, is exchanged among several of the prisoners. Finally, one of the grisly characters interrupts the silence and timidly asks, "Aren't you going to tell us what we have to do?"

Brubaker is shocked. Then he smiles and laughs. "No, this is your council. You decide what you want to do. Now, I'm busy. I have got to go in my office and make a few phone calls. You guys carry on."

Brubaker briskly disappears into his office.

Now the prisoners are really shocked. They are petrified. They don't know what to do. No one speaks. The silence drags on for a few more minutes. Finally, one of the prisoners speaks up, one of the prisoners who obviously doesn't have much use for Brubaker and his newfangled ideas. "Why don't we just forget the whole thing. We all know that The Man isn't really going to let this council do anything." The other prisoners nod in agreement.

It seems as though a weight has been lifted from them. Just as they begin to rise from their chairs to leave, Brubaker steps out of his office. "Where are you guys going? Is the meeting over? What have you decided to do?"

Again the prisoners look surprised and befuddled. They can't believe it. This guy is for real. The council is no joke. It really is going to be able to change things in the life of the prison.

The prisoners slowly sit down at the table once again. This time Brubaker sits down with them. But he doesn't sit at the head of the table. He sits off in one corner. Again there is silence, but only for a few moments.

One of the inmates blurts out, "About these dirty uniforms ..."

And so began the transformation of the prison, a transformation that was almost too good to be true. Brubaker gave those prisoners something which no other warden had ever given them: self-esteem. He thought enough of them to let them elect their own council to clean up some of the problems in the prison. Throughout the film Brubaker constantly makes the point (which ran totally contrary to the usual philosophy of the penal system) that these criminals don't respect others because they don't respect themselves. If someone showed some confidence in them, if someone would enable them to take some responsibility and gain some self-esteem, they just might start treating others better. For when you can't stand yourself, you can't stand anyone else either.

The need for self-esteem is one of the deepest and most universal of all human needs. Educators, psychologists, criminologists, and sociologists would probably all agree that when someone's dignity, sense of worth, self-image, self-esteem are taken away, his ability to function as a productive human being is severely crippled.

Why do you think abused children so often grow up to abuse their children or to become criminals? They have no self-esteem.

Do you remember the cheerful and goofy guru of weight loss, Richard Simmons? Why is he not only an advocate of weight loss but also such a cheerleader and promoter of positive thinking? You aren't going to be able to shed those pounds until you start feeling good about yourself.

Just think of someone who is successful in life? Doesn't he or she have a healthy self-image? Just think of someone who is often depressed and unhappy. Could it not be because they think so little of themselves? Without self-esteem it is so difficult to give, to love, to care, even to trust anyone else.

Jesus is not blind to this human need. Throughout his ministry, Jesus is often reaching out to fill those whose self-esteem is low. When the scribe in today's Gospel asks Jesus, "Which commandment is the first of all?" He is actually asking a question about what is most important in life. He could just as easily have asked,

"What must I do more than anything else to be happy and satisfied? What must I do to feel like somebody, to have some self-esteem?"

Jesus' answer is a quote from today's First Reading: "Love the Lord your God with all your heart, with all your soul, with all your mind, and with all your strength."

When Jesus talks about this kind of complete love of God, he is describing what it is like to trust in God no matter what, to have faith in God regardless of the circumstances. It is like a child completely believing in his parents no matter what. It is like a wife trusting completely that her husband will be faithful to her no matter what. When a wife trusts her husband, when a child can count on his parents, it gives them a sense of confidence, assurance — self-esteem. Believing that the ultimate author of all creation values and treasures even little, insignificant me can't help but give me a good self-image. And, as Brubaker proved in his prison reform, people who respect themselves will respect others.

Jesus makes a similar point when he insists that love of God is inseparable from love of neighbor. One who loves God will have a sense of self-esteem. He who has self-esteem, he who loves himself, can love his neighbor. When one believes that "God doesn't make no garbage," he won't treat other people as if they were garbage either.

But believing in God with all our heart, soul, mind, and strength is no easy task. We know that from the poor way we often treat others. When we have low self-esteem, when we do not think highly of ourselves, when we have had a bad day, when we are down in the dumps, then it is easy to strike back in anger at others. Then it is easy to cut someone else down to size with slander and gossip. When we are insecure about ourselves, that is when we need to grab all the power and success that we can. When we are unsure about ourselves, then is when we recklessly pursue one pleasure after another regardless of the consequences. We think that this is the only way to feel good about ourselves. Often the braggart and egotist is actually acting to overcome his sense of self-doubt. Maybe if he boasts enough, not only will others but perhaps even he will begin to believe that he is someone worthwhile.

This haunting voice of self-doubt and insecurity the biblical tradition and the teaching of the church has called "sin." Sin begins with our inability to love God, from the shame and self-doubt that leaves us hiding in the bushes, all too aware of our nakedness, certain of our unworthiness, just like those first sinners, Adam and Eve. The Augsburg Confession describes sin as being "without fear and love of God." Isn't that one of the ultimate consequences of hell: living without any sense of self-esteem, trapped in the depths of our despair and self-hatred? Such hell is not just in eternity. There can be "hell on earth" right now.

When we confess our sins, we are not just acknowledging that we have done something "naughty." We are not just talking about having eaten some forbidden fruit. Living in sin means that we can never seem to shed the suspicion that we are not good enough. Living in sin means that we always find the lie of the serpent making sense: "God doesn't care about you, so you had better take things into your own hands!" Living in sin means that we are eternally in search of self-esteem and never able to capture it. Living in sin means that we can never bring ourselves to trust God, to love God with all our heart, soul, mind, and strength and thereby to love our neighbors as ourselves.

The scribe seems to know all the right answers. He knows the importance of love of God and love of neighbor. Jesus compliments him for this. He is not far from the kingdom. But he is still not yet there. Something is still missing. That something is the ability to follow through. There is no person on earth who can follow through and keep this command to love God and neighbor. There is no person on earth who can do it because there is no person not tainted by the curse of Eden, because there is no person this side of Genesis 3 whose self-esteem is uncracked.

The Scriptures and the Christian tradition boldly announce to the world that this kind of self-esteem, this conviction that we are indeed somebody, even in the eyes of God, must be *given* to us. It must be *bestowed* upon us. We can only *receive* it. The mission of the church proclaims to the world that what we cannot ever seem to attain for ourselves has been given to us by God. It is a gift. It is grace.

You people sitting here this morning, this is the Good News that I have to tell you today! You can love God with all your heart, soul, mind, and strength. You can trust God. You can cling to God because he clings to you! God loves you, even though, in spite of, the doubts, the fears, the worries, the sweaty hands, the frightening dreams in the middle of the night, the cracks that seem more like fissures in your self-esteem, are always lurking around the next corner. Even though you can never shed them, God still loves you. God forgives you in spite of it all. You are the apple of his eye.

Stand up. There is no need to slump. This is no time to slouch, no time to hide in the back row, no time to try to slip away unnoticed. You are the crown of God's creation. You are his beloved sons and daughters.

Given the flaws of which we are all too aware, given the blemishes of which we are perpetually embarrassed, given the sins of which we are continually ashamed, this seems to be an incredible and outrageous claim for the church to make. It would be were it not for the one who is making this incredible claim on our behalf. He comes with the highest authorization. He is Jesus. He is God's very own Son. He is the one who comes among us to make public the secret, to reveal what has been all too hidden in the pain and ambiguity of this fallen world: God loves you and me. God forgives us. We are his beloved sons and daughters. We can have self-esteem.

There is probably no other action in the church's liturgical and worship life which so dramatically reveals that our self-esteem is purely a *gift* of God, that we don't *have to* do anything to prove ourselves, than the sacrament of Holy Baptism.

A few moments ago we baptized tiny, little Molly. Molly is an infant. She is utterly dependent. She can do nothing for herself. All she can do is eat and sleep and gurgle and laugh and cry. When water was poured over her at the font, when the name of God was spoken, it was not just the pastor acting. It was almighty God himself acting. God declared before us, before the world, and most of all before Molly that Jesus died and rose again for her.

And because of this washing with the waters of baptism, Jesus' fate is now hers. Molly has a new identity. She has a new destiny. Just like Jesus who went before her, Molly has the promise of the creator of heaven and earth. That creator will never abandon her. That creator will always love her. That creator will always welcome her. That creator is her "heavenly Father," her "daddy." Just like Jesus trusted his daddy all the way to the cross and was not disappointed, so also for Molly. Nothing or no one can ever separate her from the love of her new heavenly Father in Jesus Christ.

Because of this baptism, Molly will always be "somebody" in the eyes of God. There will never be any question that she is the apple of God's eye. This powerful promise, this eternal assurance can go a long way in comforting Molly. Every time her value is called into question, every time she doubts her self-worth, she can be reassured by what has happened here today. Molly, you are baptized! God esteems you. You can esteem yourself.

But today is only a beginning. From this day on it is the job of her parents, her sponsors, her family, her church to keep on reminding her for the rest of her life who she is, whose she is. Because of this "washing with the word" she will always be "somebody." There will be much to challenge, attack, and call into question what has been given her today. But because of her new identity, she can always be sure of who she is. She can be confident. She can have self-esteem.

Building on this new identity, she can dare to be different from those around her. She doesn't need to lust for the applause of her peers or the admiration of her neighbors. She doesn't need to be burdened by her failures. She doesn't need to hide in the back row. She doesn't need to hide in the anonymity of the crowd. Instead she can stand tall. She is righteous. She is someone she can be proud of. She is someone who can dare to love her neighbor as herself. Why? Because Jesus died for her.

And what is true for Molly is also true for us. As we are busy nurturing young saints like Molly in the promise of her baptism, we can also be about the business of reminding and reassuring one another of what God has offered us in our baptism. When that baptismal water was poured over us, we were connected to the life, death, and resurrection of Jesus. Therefore, we are somebody! We know who we are! We can have self-esteem!

If God can be this proud of us, then we surely can be proud of ourselves. We can have self-esteem.

Breaking
The Taboo

Mark 12:38-44

"**Taboo.**" **It's** a strange, mysterious, ancient-sounding word that we don't use much any more in our modern, scientifically enlightened world. A taboo is something that is forbidden. A taboo is a prohibition. It is usually associated with something sacred and mysterious. Something that is taboo is set aside, never to be touched and desecrated by human hands. We are usually afraid of the taboo. We are in awe of its power. Taboos control us. In the ancient world certain places or things may have been considered taboo. You stayed away. Hands off! In our modern world we are less likely to speak of the taboo. Nothing seems to be sacred. Nothing is forbidden. Everything is up for grabs.

But the taboos still remain. Just try to place a Christmas creche on public property. Just try to carry a confederate flag into a NAACP convention. Just try to burn a flag at the local VFW hall. Such actions desecrate the sacred. They are unthinkable, forbidden, unspeakable — taboo.

One of the biggest taboos in our society today is talking about money, and, specifically, revealing how much money one makes. People are more willing today to talk about their sex lives (which used to be taboo) than they are about how much money they make. That is the most personal and intimate of secrets. I know of families today where the children have no idea what their parents make. A friend of mine once told me that all through his college years, his father would never apply for financial aid. Why? Because in applying for financial aid he had to reveal his personal income. He ran a business. How much money he made was nobody's business but his. He wasn't about to reveal such an intimate and personal thing to a financial aid officer, someone he didn't even know. Such a thing was unthinkable, forbidden — taboo!

The church does not remain unaffected by such taboos. The subject of money is also a big taboo in the church. I have often heard people brag about their church to a friend by saying, "At our church we don't talk about money." Many times I have heard people complain when the subject of money is brought up in the church. Money seems too secular, too worldly, not spiritual enough. Some churches are so concerned about this taboo that they make a special effort in their worship services to remind any of their visitors that they are not expected to make a financial contribution when the offering plate is passed. Asking for money is too personal. It is impolite, rude, inhospitable. It is taboo.

Why is the subject of money so often taboo in the church? Some complain that such a worldly matter as money has no place in the spiritual business of the church. That could hardly be further from the truth. The truth of the matter is that there is probably nothing in our society that is as spiritual and religious a matter as the subject of money. If you want to find out what people truly value in life, look at their checkbook. If you want to see what someone is truly loyal to, what one truly trusts, then examine how they spend their money.

As Martin Luther reminds us in his explanation to the first commandment in his *Large Catechism,* whatever one most trusts, values, is loyal to, that is his god. There is no such thing as an atheist because everyone has someone or something that gives his life meaning. That is his god. Therefore, if our use of money reflects our ultimate values and commitments, what we trust, what is our god, then there is nothing that is more religiously and spiritually revealing than the subject of money.

The problem is that we don't want to be put under the microscope. We don't want to have anyone asking such "personal" questions about our "real" religion. Such talking about money in church is taboo.

The truth is that all of us much of the time are busy trusting other gods than the god of Jesus. Just look at how we spend our money. Just look at what we are really committed to. It isn't very pretty. It isn't very faithful.

The subject of money may be taboo in the church, but it certainly wasn't taboo for Jesus. Continually in his preaching and teaching Jesus breaks the taboo. When Jesus talks about the kingdom of God he uses images and illustrations from the world of money and economics more than any other. Jesus is continually talking about money. The little story of "the widow's mite" (as it has often been called in the church) in today's gospel is one such example. At the heart of this illustration is money. From Jesus' perspective there is no better way to talk about one's relationship to God.

Jesus sat near the temple treasury and watched the crowds go by making their contributions. The money was placed in a trumpet-shaped opening which led to the container below. The more coins you put in, the more noise you would make — and the more attention you would draw to yourself. Many would call this "sounding the trumpet." This is the same kind of image that is behind the modern way we refer to someone who is calling attention to themselves: "They are tooting their own horn."

You can be sure that the rich often liked to make a lot of noise when they made their contributions. It made them look good. And you can be sure that the fund-raisers in the temple would have also made much of all the noise and would have invited others to join in. But Jesus surprises everyone by calling their attention not to the large and noisy and attention-getting gifts of the rich but to the small and silent gift of the poor widow. Even though the sound she created in the trumpet would have been barely audible, even though her contribution was only one cent, it was far greater than all the noise of the big bucks. Why? Because she gave everything she had.

This story has long been a favorite of "stewardship programs" in the church. This story has been used to try to motivate people to give more money to the church. The poor widow has been cited as an example of the value of percentage giving. Even though the rich may actually give more money, what is more important is the percentage of your income that you give to the church. From that perspective the widow actually gave a higher percentage of her money. And that is the example Jesus wants us to follow.

Unfortunately, such an interpretation skips an important detail. The widow didn't just give a percentage of her income to the temple. She gave everything she had — 100 percent.

On second thought, maybe she isn't such a good example when it comes to raising money for the church. If there is someone who would scare off potential donors, it is this widow. She is a strange lady. She is dangerous. She gives everything she has to the temple treasury. Does her example mean that we should be willing to give all our money to the church? Or does her example mean something else? Maybe her example isn't about increasing our percentage giving to the church budget at all?

Maybe the point is this: This woman had a better understanding of her relationship to God than all those rich people who loved to sound the trumpet with their big offerings or those scribes and other religious leaders who were criticized in this passage by Jesus. Those scribes were the experts in determining just how much one ought to give to the temple. They were the experts in computing the tithe, and deciding just how much to give to God and how much to keep for oneself. But they had it all wrong. The widow had it all right. She recognized that her use of her money was never a case of giving some of it back to God and keeping the rest for herself. All of it already belongs to God.

It is arrogant, presumptuous, and sinful to think that we can give some of our money back to God in our church offering and keep the rest for ourselves. It is all God's. And this poor widow is recognizing that fact through her simple gift.

What makes her example so troubling is that she is willing to recognize what the rest of us resist doing. She completely trusts God with her life, her whole life, not just a percentage of it. Such trust continually escapes us.

We live in a much different world. We live in a world in the grips of the great taboo. We live in a world that is forbidden to question or challenge the great taboo. To challenge this taboo is to question the most basic assumption and belief of our world. And that is forbidden — taboo.

And what is that great taboo? What is the unspeakable power that holds us hostage? That we live in a world of scarcity; that we live in a world of limitations; that there is only so much wealth to go around. Therefore, you have either got to hold on to and preserve the wealth you have or work hard at creating more wealth. Either way, we live under the threat of scarcity. Either way, we live in fear of not having enough. We live life trusting the power of the almighty dollar. We live life believing that finally even God is going to judge us on the basis of our ability to be good stewards of our money. We believe that the size of our bank account ultimately determines who we are. We are held hostage.

That is why the behavior of the widow is so troubling. She breaks the taboo. She has no fear of not having enough. She is totally oblivious to the threat of scarcity. She trusts a future in which she obviously believes there will always be abundance. She does not determine her value by the size of her bank account because she is willing to give it all away.

Jesus called everyone's attention to the example of this poor widow because she exemplified what he was all about. Jesus also lived his life breaking the taboo. Jesus came to shatter the taboo that everyone assumed was true about life and money and God. Jesus dared to call the creator of heaven and earth "Abba," Father, Daddy. Jesus dared to believe that his father loved him abundantly, without limit, even though he had nothing. Jesus refused to be afraid of scarcity. He didn't need to prove himself by the size of his bank account. Instead he trusted the abundant promises of God. Instead of trying to accumulate for himself, he gave himself away without regard for his own financial well-being. Like this poor widow, in spite of appearances to the contrary, in spite of the world's definition of wealth and status, Jesus believed he was rich. Therefore, he was able to give himself away for the sake of others. Like that widow, he gave everything that he had. He gave his whole life away, all the way to death on the cross.

And most of all Jesus dared to announce to the world that this desire to love the world, to give himself away, to sacrifice everything that he had, was the very nature of God. Yes, breaking the taboo that had so enslaved this world in fear, Jesus announces that

61

God can be trusted because God loves, because God is merciful, because God forgives, abundantly, without limit, eternally. There is no need to fear scarcity. God's love will never run out. There will always be plenty.

People, this is good news to a world that is held hostage to the great taboo. The church announces that in Jesus Christ God has broken the great taboo. The church's ministry is always seeking to reflect this incredible abundance that knows no end.

The sacrament of Baptism is only administered once in a person's life. There is no need ever to do it again. Why? Because the gift of Baptism knows no limit. There is never a scarcity of God's love. This is a promise that lasts forever.

As we gather to eat and drink around this table, we eat a fore-taste of the feast to come. We can look forward to eating one day at a table covered with unlimited abundance. There is no end to the love offered at this table. God will never take it away.

And believe it or not, money is no longer the big taboo. We are not afraid to talk about it. We are not afraid to recognize it for what it is, i.e., a reflection of our values and beliefs, of our religion. And because we believe that we live in the kingdom of God, in this new world of unlimited abundance, because we are no longer held hostage to the power of money, we can dare to give that money away in an offering for the sake of others. There is no need to be stingy. There is no need to worry about getting something in return.

Breaking the taboo of money also means that we don't let the tremendous emphasis our society puts on money control us. There is more to life than money. Likewise, there is more to stewardship than money. Living in this new kingdom economy of abundance means that this new sense of generosity and sacrifice will affect not only the use of our money but also everything that we do with our lives. Given this new world of abundance and plenty, we now get to live our lives no longer imprisoned by the old taboo, always having to worry about what's in it for me. Rather, the focus of our lives can be on others and their needs. We can give everything that we have, our whole lives, like that widow outside the temple and like Jesus in his journey to the cross to God.

And where can we do that? Where do we love God? Not just in giving time and money to the church but also in giving ourselves in love to our neighbor, wherever we come in contact with people in our daily lives.

Occasionally I am just gratified to see this sense of generosity and service show up in the lives of the people of this congregation. It shows me that at times we can break the taboo. At times we actually can live our lives trusting the abundance of God and daring to give ourselves away for the sake of others.

I have always found it gratifying to hear the young people of our congregation, as they plan what to do with their lives when they graduate from high school, speak not just of having a career that will make them lots of money, but also of doing something with their lives that will make this world a better place. Because of the power of the gospel, they are daring to believe the abundant promises of God. They are daring to trust the love of God. They are daring to live as if there is more to life than the accumulation of money. They are daring to trust God's gift of abundance and reject the world's lie of scarcity. They are beginning to break the taboo.

So can you, as you discover the same privilege that widow did that day at the temple treasury. You live in a world of unlimited abundance. And you can give it away in the service of God and the love of your neighbor.

Judgment Day

Mark 13:1-8

Introductory Drama

Characters: Man
　　　　　　　Woman

(Scene: The entrance to eternity. A man sits at a desk, papers before him. Woman enters. She goes to the man and stands quietly. The man looks up.)

Man: Heaven on your right — hell on your left.

Woman: *(Looking at the doors, in awe)* You mean that door leads to heaven ... and that one to hell?

Man: That is correct. Please don't take too long. There are others waiting.

Woman: But ... what do I do?

Man: You go through one of them.

Woman: You mean I have the choice?

Man: That is correct.

Woman: *(Craftily)* Oh, well, I'll take heaven.

Man: *(Motioning)* Over there, please.

Woman: Well, thanks ... *(She starts toward heaven gleefully. As she is about to go through the door, she stops a moment. She turns and comes back)* Now look. I don't want to make any mistakes at a time like this. You're giving me my choice ... I can go to heaven or to hell. That's what you said, isn't it?

Man: That is correct.

Woman: I mean, if I choose heaven, it's not some sort of ... er ... test or something? There are no strings attached?

Man: There are no strings attached.

Woman: *(Relieved)* I had no idea it would be like this. Well, thanks ... *(She starts toward heaven. She hesitates, then comes back)* Now I don't want you to think just because I choose heaven that I've always been a model of good behavior ... *(Hastily)* I haven't always been perfect. Who has? *(She laughs as though sharing a joke)* I'm not trying to get out of anything.

Man: I understand.

Woman: All right, then. Just so long as it's clear. *(She starts toward heaven. Hesitates. Comes back)* Er ... pardon me ...

Man: Yes?

Woman: I mean, once I go in there, I *stay* there.

Man: You stay there.

Woman: I mean this *is* ... er ... Judgment Day?

Man: This is Judgment Day.

Woman: And once I make my decision, it's final ...

Man: Final.

Woman: I don't believe it! That's not the way it is at all! The righteous go to heaven and are rewarded for their goodness ... The wicked go to hell and are punished for their sins! Ask anybody!

Man: Please don't take too long. There are others waiting.

Woman: But this is idiotic! Doesn't everybody choose heaven?

Man: Some.

Woman: Look, have I got it wrong? In heaven the streets are paved with gold, isn't that so?

Man: That is correct.

Woman: And hell is a burning pit where you burn forever. Isn't that right?

Man: That is correct.

Woman: Then I fail to understand why anyone would choose to ... *(She starts toward heaven. Hesitates, come back)* What's going on here? Don't you know I've lived all my life in fear of this day with the view of getting into heaven and cheating hell? What are you trying to get away with around here? I demand a fair trial!

Man: No trial.

Woman: You mean to sit there and tell me this is Judgment Day and there's no trial?

Man: That is correct.

Woman: This is outrageous! I demand a hearing! My father pulled a trick like this on me once and I never forgave him. I was in the fifth grade. I skipped school one day. I came home later and he asked me where I'd been. I told him I'd been in school. I lied to him. He said the school had called up and asked where I was. I wasn't there. So I told him the truth ... I confessed ... I told him I'd lied and everything! And what did he do? He *grinned* at me and went back to his paper! *(Savagely)* What kind of business is that? He should have taken that strap and beaten me within an inch of my life! *(More angry)* Now I come up here ... Judgment Day ... ready to pay for my sins ... *(She beats on the table)* I want a hearing! I demand a trial!

Man: No trial. Please don't take too long.

Woman: It's not fair ... you can't do this to me ... I'm innocent ... I never had the chance other people had ... I've had a hard life ... I didn't mean to do anything bad ... give me just one more chance ... *(She starts running to the door into hell)* Please ...

Man: There are others waiting.

Woman: Father! Father! Help me! *(She runs out of the door into hell)*

Man: *(Looking up)* Next, please.

* * *

After seeing this little drama, we wonder how she could have done it. What was the matter with her? Didn't she see the light? How could she have turned her back on something that was so obvious? She had every opportunity to choose heaven. Yet, somehow, she couldn't help herself. She really didn't want to go to hell — yet she couldn't seem to do anything else.

Heaven without a trial? Heaven without an opportunity to prove herself? It just didn't seem right. It's not what she expected. It's just too shocking to be true. Everything gets turned upside down.

Nothing is as it should be. Right becomes wrong. Good becomes evil. And yes, as we just saw, heaven becomes hell.

We wouldn't have made the same mistake, would we? Or would we?

I hope this little drama has helped to reveal how shocking God's ways are when compared to our human sensibilities. If we are really honest with ourselves, we must admit that we would have had just as difficult a time as the girl in the drama when it comes to accepting the way that God wants to deal with us. We and so much of the church with us have a very difficult time believing that God could be so gracious and merciful. And so, we look for substitutes, for ways to pay for our sins, to earn a hearing, to get a fair trial, because ultimately, deep down in our hearts, we believe that we have earned our piece of heaven.

But God's ways are not our ways. His thoughts are not our thoughts. He turns our world upside down and inside out. What we think is important, valuable, strong, and enduring is trivial in the eyes of God. And what we think is weak, foolish, and insignificant is in the eyes of God powerful, wise, and important.

A popular tourist attraction in Washington, D.C., is the magnificent National Cathedral. This great structure is indeed a sight to behold. It is immense, imposing, enduring. Why do so many come to visit? Maybe because in this world of disposable diapers, non-returnable soft drink bottles, throw-away cartons, biodegradable shopping bags, and plastic everything, it is reassuring to encounter something so substantial. So much that surrounds us is too transitory, here today and gone tomorrow. Everything changes, decays, and is tossed on the garbage heap of history. But the National Cathedral, eternal-looking, immense and imposing, with stone upon stone, arch upon arch — it surely shall last. Or so it seems.

In today's Gospel we meet "tourists" of another time, the disciples, who were walking by the temple one day in Jerusalem, admiring its massive beauty. So many stones. Arches upon arches. But when the disciples shared their admiration with Jesus, he did not respond with the same enthusiasm. Instead he said, "Do you see these great buildings? Not one stone will be left here upon another; all will be thrown away."

69

It must have been difficult for the disciples to conceive that Herod's great temple, one of the wonders of the ancient world, would be torn down, stone by stone, until it was nothing but a heap of rubble. Such a thing was unimaginable. The temple, the very center of national life and pride, the very seat of God, destroyed? Unthinkable!

Yet, that is what Jesus told the disciples about this supposedly eternal temple of God, and barely forty years after he spoke these words, it would lay in ruin. Jesus' words came true: "For nation will rise against nation, and kingdom against kingdom; there will be earthquakes in various places, there will be famines."

We are not used to hearing such talk in our churches these days. Today many of us want a religion that will affirm and confirm the present order and current world rather than a religion that will speak of the future and Judgment Day and the end of this world as we know it.

In the last generation the churches have become increasingly aware of the fragility of life in this world. Even though many have said that we no longer face the same dangers with the fall of communism in Eastern Europe and the Soviet Union, we still live in a world that is very dangerous.

We hear of numerous third world nations, Iraq most recently, trying to improve their status in the world by building their own nuclear weapons. I recently read an absolutely frightening description of what might happen in a nuclear attack that could devastate not only this country but much of the world. There would be an "incredible firestorm in which hundreds of tons of sooty smoke would absorb so much of the sun's rays that only five percent of the normal amount of light would reach the earth ... all land plants would be damaged or destroyed ... temperature would plummet for several months ... all biological life on the planet would be gravely threatened."

Such a description makes me shudder and I begin to wonder if the end of this world isn't all that far away. Add to that all the concerns about the environmental problems we are creating (air pollution, depletion of the ozone layer, global warming, and so on) and it is easy to start thinking of giving up.

But there is a strange irony in all of this. The supporters of nuclear weapons and the critics, the environmentalists and the disciples of big business, the hawks and the doves, all have one fundamental assumption in common: Survival of this world and this life is all that matters. Fearful about the water we drink, the air we breathe, the great mushroom cloud looming over our heads, we get by as best we can and grab what we can. And when we are very frightened, we tend to hold on very tightly — even to the things that do not last.

That's why Jesus' words in today's Gospel are so unwelcome. When he was asked about possibilities for the future, about prospects for tomorrow, Jesus responded frankly, saying that there will be an end, stones cast down, famine, terrors, wars, nation rising against nation. But what does Jesus really mean? The doomsayers and prophets of nuclear holocaust or environmental disaster would have us believe that Jesus' words may be fulfilled very soon.

On the other hand, we might be tempted to believe that Jesus was wrong. The world did not come to an end during Jesus' generation. The temple was destroyed in 70 A.D. and the Roman empire did eventually fall, but the world did not come to end. Even Saint Paul told early Christians not to marry, not to worry about whether they were slaves or free because this world was soon to end, but it didn't. Was Paul wrong too?

No. Quite the contrary. At the heart of our Christian faith is the belief that *we have already seen the end.* In a sense the end of the world has already happened. Judgment Day has already occurred in the life, death, and resurrection of Jesus Christ. In his death and resurrection the entire history of the earth has reached its turning point. At that moment, when he was nailed to the cross, the end of history took place. A new kingdom was established, a kingdom not dependent on whether we work out a mutually verifiable arms treaty with all the third world countries of the world, prevent the spread of weapons of mass destruction, replenish the ozone layer, or halt global warming.

In today's Gospel Jesus tells us not to be alarmed, not to be frightened. We don't have to be afraid of the dangerous uncertainties of this world. We don't have to be afraid of nuclear holocaust or environmental disaster or cancer or AIDS or an auto accident or a recession. We have already experienced Judgment Day. We know how it is going to end up. Therefore we don't have to worry about saving ourselves, our skins, our investments, our possessions, our world.

At the close of today's Gospel Jesus compares this fact to the beginning of the pangs of birth. When a mother begins that painful ordeal of childbirth, there are times when she may feel defeated. The pain is too great. The suffering is too much. But what keeps her going is the promise and expectation of that new life. What keeps her going is the blessed assurance that every other mother has given her. On the basis of their experience she can have peace and confidence. She knows that the blessed birth is about to take place.

Right now it may look like the world is going to hell in a handbasket. The future may not look bright. Danger seems to be around every corner. But we have the blessed assurance that the final outcome has already been determined. Judgment Day has already happened. God's love will triumph.

We get ourselves into trouble when the things of this world become ultimately important. When our survival in this world is all that matters, then we are inclined to accept all sorts of lesser evils. Remember, Jesus was put to death by a politician who just wanted to preserve law and order in Jerusalem. Remember, it was Caiaphas, the high priest, who noted that one man's death was not too great a price to pay for peace in our time.

Jesus once said, "My peace I give to you, not as the world gives peace." This is the peace that God gives to us in Jesus Christ, peace which is showered upon us in the waters of Baptism and offered to us in the bread and wine of Holy Communion. Only God can give us this peace, for it is based on the promise from God himself that it is not our job to make history come out right or to save the world or to write the last chapter of history, because in Jesus Christ history has already come out right. The world has already been saved. The last chapter has already been written. In Jesus Christ we have already seen the end. Judgment Day has already happened.

That doesn't mean we should throw in the towel in this world and give up. We can and should still work for peace, for the environment, for a safer and cleaner society, because this is still God's world and through us he still loves it. But we can do it without fear, without living under the burden that it all depends on us. We know where it is all headed. And Jesus has promised to give us his Holy Spirit so that we can be confident about it and be able to speak the truth about what is right and wrong and good and evil and where there is genuine hope and what can be trusted. There will be no confusion of heaven and hell. We know that our hope lies only in the promise of God. It is precisely our foolish trust in our own places, devices, and schemes which turns this world of God's into a living hell both now and forever.

Perhaps some of you remember General Alexander Haig, a great military leader in the war in Vietnam and political leader in the Reagan administration. Now, General Haig was not exactly what you would call a great theologian. He once said something which on the surface sounded utterly stupid, and he was roundly criticized by the media for saying it. He said, "There are worse things than a nuclear war."

That sounds like he stuck his foot in his mouth, but that is exactly what we Christians believe. What is far worse than a nuclear war? Not having faith and trust in God. Not to trust God and his promises means that we are headed for a destiny even worse than a nuclear holocaust.

But to trust and believe the promises of God means that nothing in this world, not even the mushroom cloud of a nuclear bomb or the ecological disaster of global warming or the insidious attack of terminal cancer or the suffering and humiliation of an economic recession can separate us from the love of God in Jesus Christ.

We can believe that because our Judgment Day has already happened. And we will no longer confuse heaven and hell.

When The
Fat Lady Sings

Mark 13:24-32

That great twentieth century prophet of Yankee Stadium, Yogi Berra, said it well when describing the uncertainty of any athletic contest: "It ain't over 'til it's over." Until that last fly ball is caught or strike is called or ground ball is thrown to first base and the last out is made, the game is not over. Anything can happen. And more often than not it has. Everyone has a story about dramatic comebacks in the bottom half of the ninth inning.

I suppose that is why Red Auerbach, the former great coach of the Boston Celtics, used to irritate so many of his opponents when he would lean back and light up that huge cigar. It was Red's way of announcing his confidence. Even though there would be time left on the clock, he was sure that the game was as good as over and his Celtics would win. As he leaned back puffing on his cigar even while the players still raced up and down the court, he knew it was over. Such arrogance piqued his opponents and delighted his fans.

I think it originated in some eastern ballpark a generation or so ago. I'm not sure of its exact origins. You still see fans expressing the sentiment today on large banners and posters which they love to flash for the television cameras. It expresses the eternal optimism of sports fans who are unwilling to give up until the last out is made or the clock has finally run out: "It's not over until the fat lady sings." And the fat lady hasn't sung. Therefore there is still hope. Their team can still pull it out. Of course, the same phrase is reversed by the team whose fans are confident that victory is theirs and want to rub it in to the opposition: "The fat lady has started to sing."

When the last out is made and the final buzzer sounds, it's over. "The fat lady sings." There is no changing what has happened. The game gets chalked up as a win or loss.

There is a sense of finality to an athletic contest. There are clear winners and losers. When it's over, it's over. I suppose that is one of the things that makes athletic contests so appealing. There is a sense of finality, a sense of clarity about them. When the NCAA champ is crowned, when the Super Bowl is over, when the World Series is finished, there is no question about who is the best. It's over. Final. Complete. Finished. There is a winner and there is a loser. So much in life lacks this sense of finality. Few things ever come to closure. It always gets dragged out until tomorrow. There are always shades of gray and little that is black and white. Questions always remain unanswered. Life is filled with ambiguity. It gets frustrating. We wish that someone would draw the line. We wish that someone would settle the score. We wish that someone would set things right. We wonder if this will all ever come to an end or if life is an endless circle, eternally spinning with no sense of direction, the same things happening over and over again, something without beginning and without end. Maybe the fat lady will never sing.

The universe seems to have been around for billions of years. It could be around for billions more years. These numbers are mind-numbing when you think that humans have only been recording history for five or six thousand years.

I remember a conversation I had with my father many years ago. I must have been a small child who was shocked by the cruel treatment I had received from my friends. He reminded me how I shouldn't be surprised. People are sinners. The more things change, the more they stay the same, when it comes to human nature. "There is nothing new under the sun."

Perhaps that is why Jesus' words in today's Gospel seem so unreal, almost farfetched. Almost 2,000 years ago Jesus spoke graphically of the end of the world. The universe will literally fall apart and he will return riding on the clouds in all of his glory for the final judgment. He will finally set things right. The bad guys will finally get what they had coming to them. The good guys, here called "the elect," will finally get saved. Finally, at last, there will be some closure on human history. Finally, the last out will be made and the final buzzer will sound. Finally, there will be clear winners and losers. Finally, the fat lady will sing!

But that was 2,000 years ago. We are still waiting. I can just hear Yogi Berra reminding us, "It's not over 'til it's over." Most of us go on living our lives as if the end will never come. There will always be a tomorrow. If anyone seriously thinks that the end is coming or that the end is near, then we are ready to call the men in the white coats to take them to the nearest psychiatric hospital. People who take seriously Jesus' words in today's Gospel, who believe that the end is near, who warn us of the impending judgment of the world, are either ignored or ridiculed as a bunch of religious fanatics. When we think of people who have a vivid sense of the end of the world, we think of people like Jim Jones or Ted Kazcynski or some survivalist sect in the wilderness of Montana stockpiling weapons for the impending day of doom or some weird religious commune in which everyone commits suicide in order to be saved before Halley's Comet or some other intergalactic missile crashes into the earth.

In other words, when it comes to the words like today's Gospel, either Jesus was mistaken about the end of the world or he was talking about something else. Either way, we along with the rest of the world go on living our lives as if the fat lady will never sing.

But like that pesky fly who keeps buzzing in the bedroom and disturbing our nap, there always seem to be those interruptions, these disturbing surprises that jolt us of our routines, reminding us that our lives will not go on forever, that there very may well be that day when the fat lady sings.

That lump in your breast, the blood in the toilet bowl, the shortness of breath, the sagging muscles and graying hair, they all remind us that the end is getting closer. The cosmos may not be falling apart but our lives will one day fall apart. There is nothing we can do about that.

A friend of mine once said, "Life is dangerous. It can kill you." And eventually it does. No one gets out alive!

And it may not just be our health. All too often I have seen people who are in the pink of health but whose world and universe are literally falling apart. A wife is devastated when her husband one day announces that he is filing for divorce. He has fallen in love with someone else. The high school football team has been working hard for months to win the big game against their archrival, but they lose. They have failed. And to those players, slouching on the bench, some with tears washing the mud off their cheeks, it is the end of the world. More than once I have seen middle-aged men, who seem to have had the world by the tail and were on top of their careers, reduced to blubbering shadows of themselves, egos destroyed, haunted by self-doubt, devastated, because they had become another casualty of the latest corporate merger. For them the fat lady has sung.

For a modern and enlightened world that doesn't believe that there will ever be an end, we do an awful lot of worrying about the end. The millennium is approaching and fears about the Y2K problem, global warming, and nuclear terrorism are popping up all over the place. The future seems to stand or fall on the basis of what Alan Greenspan utters or on the forecasts of the latest stock market analyst. Some people say their prayers before they go to sleep at night. Others won't close their eyes until they have consulted their bedside astrologer. Late night television is filled with the testimonials of those whose lives have been given new hope and direction because they have had a psychic reading of their future.

It may not be over until the fat lady sings. But the world is convinced that one day she will sing and it had better be ready.

Jesus' vivid description of the last day in today's Gospel may at first glance seem fantastic and farfetched. But upon further review, it may not seem as fantastic and farfetched as we had thought. Whether the fat lady sings at our next breath or next hour or next week or next month or next year or next century or next millennium, it ultimately doesn't make all that much difference to you and me. Whether the cosmos or just our personal lives go up in flames, it doesn't make any difference. The point is this: we are afraid that we won't be ready when the fat lady sings.

It should come as no surprise then that Jesus' disciples and friends are constantly questioning him about when that time will arrive. They want to know when the fat lady will sing. But Jesus steadfastly resists giving them any kind of timetable. When he does speak of the signs of the end, the signs are so vague and general that they are of no use. Any attempt to figure out a timetable for the last day, whether on the basis of Jesus' words or the bizarre imagery of the Book of Revelation, is futile. As Jesus reminds us in today's Gospel, not even he knows when the fat lady will sing. Only the Father knows.

The question is not *if* the fat lady will sing. The question is *when* she will sing.

If that is the case, then why does Jesus hint that these things will happen within the lifetime of the current generation? He may not know the exact minute and hour, but he does have a general sense of its nearness. And it's definitely not hundreds of years off in the distant future. The same could be said for Saint Paul and many of the early Christians. At one point they too believed that Jesus was going to return and bring down the curtain on history in their lifetime. But after 2,000 years it still hasn't happened. No wonder we wonder if the fat lady will ever sing.

Some scholars have argued that Jesus wasn't really mistaken. We just have failed to understand him. Jesus wasn't referring to the end of the world but to the fall of Jerusalem and the destruction of the temple in 70 A.D. That experience was disastrous for the Jewish people. For them it was the ending of their world and everything in which they believed.

But such an interpretation still doesn't take Jesus' words at face value. It assumes that Jesus' talk about the end of the world has meaning for individuals and their personal lives but says nothing about the end of the cosmos and the judgment of the universe. In other words, the world may have ended for the Jews of Jerusalem in 70 A.D. Our world might come to an end when we breathe our last, whenever that is, but the universe goes on. The stars keep burning, the planets rotating. The galaxies keep expanding. Life goes on infinitely, forever. Nothing really changes.

Maybe my father was right. "The more things change, the more they stay the same."

It is tempting to believe this way. I suspect that this is the way many of us try to make sense of the universe. But it is wrong. It is the perspective of unfaith. It is the resignation of someone who no longer trusts the promises of God.

Jesus literally meant what he said. It was no metaphor or figure of speech. He did not intend to mean something other than what he actually said. Jesus expected the end to come in "this generation." And it did.

If the Last Day, the end of the world, means the final and ultimate judgment of the whole universe, then that has already happened. It happened when Jesus was nailed to the cross, when he suffered and died. It happened when Jesus was raised from the dead three days later. It happened when Jesus was ascended into heaven to take his seat at the right hand of the Father. This is the incredible message of the gospel. God was in Jesus Christ reconciling the world to himself. God was in Jesus Christ executing his final judgment on the world. And because Jesus trusted the promises of his Father, even unto his death, he was raised from the dead.

The Church has this wonderful message to announce to the world: Because of what Jesus Christ did, God has executed his final judgment on the world. Because of Jesus, we are acquitted of our sin. Because of Jesus we are forgiven, set free from the powers of death and evil and granted eternal life.

But that message remains "hidden" in the simple words, humble sacraments, and ordinary deeds of compassion carried out in the church. That message is promised now to be believed by faith against the appearances of a world where it seems that the endless cycle of sin and death will continue forever. What now remains hidden, what now is believed by faith and not by sight, will one day, on the Last Day, be revealed to all. Then it will be clear to all, even to those who have chosen not to believe, that Jesus was who he claimed to be. Then it will be clear to all in the heavens above and on the earth below that Jesus was right. God is gracious and merciful. God can be trusted. God will keep his promises to those who have trusted him.

On that day not only will our lives be different, but also life will be different for the entire cosmos. The universe as we have known it will come to end. And there will be a new heaven and a new earth. On that day all will be set right. On that day there will be no longer any doubts or questions. It will be clear to all. The fat lady has begun to sing. It's over.

In the meantime, we live in a world marked by a sense of the *already but not yet*. By faith we trust that our final destiny has *already* been determined for us in Jesus Christ. But the final arrival of that fate has *not yet* come. So, we live "between the times," the time of our personal salvation and the time of the salvation of the universe.

It is like being awake during those precious few minutes before dawn. The sky is still dark, but you are confident that the sun's first rays will eventually begin coming over the horizon. You are confident that in the next hour a new day will finally come. And there is nothing that can change that.

It is like being present at the moment of childbirth. Despite the pain, the parents live with the certain hope that new birth, new life, a new beginning is about to happen.

It is like that fig tree to which Jesus refers in today's Gospel. It may be the dead of winter, but the signs of new life are upon us. As that tree becomes tender and puts forth its first new shoots, we are sure and certain that summer is near. We wait with hope, between the times, already knowing that the summer has begun even though it has not yet actually arrived.

I once heard a preacher describe the battle of New Orleans as an example of what it is like to live "between the times," in the already but not yet, with the certain hope that when the fat lady sings, it will be a glorious day. Andrew Jackson fought and won the battle of New Orleans some days after the Treaty of Ghent had actually been signed, bringing to an end the hostilities between the U. S. and England. Jackson's side had already won, but the battle was fought anyway because there were still existing "pockets of resistance" which had not yet received the news of the treaty. So also do we fight on against the "pockets of resistance" which challenge the victory of God, whose treaty was signed at Calvary and the empty tomb. The evidence of God's victory may not always be clear. But we live "by faith." We believe against the evidence. We trust the promise of the Gospel.

When we gather around the font to baptize in the name of the Father, Son, and Holy Spirit, that baptismal candidate is already experiencing the final judgment. That person is already experiencing the last chapter of his life as he dies and rises with Christ. The fat lady has sung.

When we gather around the table to eat and drink the body and blood of our Lord, we are eating and drinking with all the saints of every time and place, with Abraham and Moses and Isaiah, with Peter and James and Paul, with Grandpa and Grandma and all those who have trusted the promises of God. When that bread and wine touch our lips, it is also Jesus touching us, welcoming us home at the final judgment. The fat lady has sung.

In the meantime we live with hope. Those unexpected interruptions in life may threaten us and call into question our future. But we do not need to be afraid. Jesus has given us his promise. And Jesus reminds us that even though heaven and earth might pass away, his words will never pass away. He keeps his promises. Our future is in his gracious hands.

Let the fat lady sing!

Telling
The Truth

John 8:31-36

You catch your child with his hand in the cookie jar just after you have told him, "Hands off!" But instead of a confession all you hear are excuses: "But, Dad, I thought you said I could have one."

Terror strikes in your heart as you suddenly look up in your rear view mirror and see those flashing red lights. "But, officer, I'm sure I wasn't going over the speed limit!"

The recent fiasco surrounding the White House has been met with such comments as, "Everyone lies about having an affair. It's no big deal." And the already questionable credibility of politicians has slid even further down the tube as President Clinton insists that "is" does not really mean "is" and that "alone" does not really mean "alone."

You would think that telling the truth would not be all that difficult. But as we all know, life can be confusing and complicated. Our own motives often remain hidden and unrecognized, even to ourselves. And most of all, we are often not as innocent as we would like to be. It is not easy to tell the truth. We would rather offer excuses and denials and equivocations.

That is also the problem at the center of today's Gospel. You would think that Jesus would be more congenial to those Jews who had shown some interest in him. But he gives it to them with both barrels. He accuses them not only of not telling the truth but also of refusing to recognize the truth when it is right before their eyes.

Jesus says, "If you continue in my word, you are truly my disciples; and you will know the truth and the truth will make you free." In other words, Jesus was saying to these Jews, who were proud of their ethnic heritage, their religion, and their grasp of the truth, that they don't know the truth. And because they don't know the truth, they can't recognize the truth about themselves. And the truth about themselves is that they are not free at all. They are slaves — to sin.

Of course, these Jews, who probably expected Jesus to treat them better (after all, they had been respectfully listening to what Jesus had to say), were not too happy with what Jesus had to say about them. They were descendants of Abraham. They were part of a proud ethnic tradition. Their genes guaranteed their status as God's chosen people. They had maintained their race and their religion for centuries in the face of often brutal oppression and persecution. They were free and slaves to no one. How could Jesus ever think they were not free, let alone call them slaves?

But Jesus heaps more coals on the fire. Because these Jews still sin, they are slaves. They are imprisoned. They have no freedom at all. It's not just that they make a few little mistakes or errors in judgment. They are enslaved to the power of sin and cannot free themselves. This is the truth they cannot accept.

Like those first century Jews, we don't want to face the truth, let alone tell the truth. Like those first century Jews, we are proud of our heritage. We are Americans. This is the cradle of democracy. This is the land of the free and the home of the brave. We are free. We are enslaved to no one. We are citizens of the world's one remaining superpower. But the truth of the matter is that we, like those first century Jews, are slaves. We are enslaved and cannot free ourselves.

When you think about it, it really takes a lot of nerve for the church to talk this way in America at the close of the twentieth century. This is the land of free markets. The cold war is over and won by us. Our economy has enjoyed its longest uninterrupted expansion ever. This is the land of the Bill of Rights. In fact, everyone has rights — and don't you step on my rights or I will sue you!

Oh, we might make a few mistakes or errors in judgment. We may have our weaknesses. We may occasionally fail. But sin?

Sin? That sounds just too harsh, too impolite, too judgmental. Don't you dare shove your morality down my throat. I have rights! I am free! I can do as I please!

But the truth of the matter is that we are not as free as we like to think. Always having to "keep up with the Joneses," always having to have the latest computer or electronic gadget, the latest SUV, the latest style of jeans or cut of hair — I would hardly call that freedom. It seems that the great cultural orthodoxy to which we must all conform and which we dare not question is that we must always have more and more, always have the latest, the newest, the fastest, the hippest, the smartest. Are we free to consume, or are we enslaved to consumerism?

And are we really free to do as we please? The sexual revolution of the last generation would like us to believe that. But has this unfettered freedom really brought us such great blessings? The deadly spectres of AIDS and sexually transmitted diseases and abortion and shattered marriages and broken families signal that this freedom has been more a curse than a blessing. The supposed freedom has only revealed how much we still are enslaved to our selfish appetites.

Paul's impassioned lament suddenly sounds very contemporary: "The good that I want to do, I do not do. And the evil I do not want to do is what I do."

And Jesus answered them, "Very truly, I tell you, everyone who commits a sin is a slave to sin." Timely words even for the end of the millennium in the land of freedom.

The truth is not pretty. The truth is not going to be popular. The latest pollsters are not going to find high approval ratings for such talk. This is not the kind of stuff that is going to sell and make you successful. Nevertheless, it is the truth. And it is truth that the church is called to speak. And Jesus surprisingly, paradoxically, amazingly thinks that such truth-telling is ultimately going to set the world free.

Today on this Reformation Sunday we remember that great reforming movement of the sixteenth century begun by Martin Luther which literally tore up the Christian Church in Europe. At the time of the Reformation, Luther attacked the church and demanded change because the church was no longer telling people the truth! Instead the church was peddling a conglomeration of lies and half-truths which ultimately undermined and corrupted its very essence.

In a sense the church is *an island of truth in a sea of lies!* The truth which the church has to announce to the world is twofold, two-sided, double-edged. The truth is this: On the one hand, as Jesus says in today's Gospel, we are slaves to sin. We are trapped, broken, evil, perverse, and at odds with God! And despite our best intentions, we can't help being anything different. But on the other hand, there is another truth. Jesus is the Christ, "the one sent from the Father." Look at Jesus and you see what God is really like: gracious and merciful, even though we do not deserve it. This is the truth, the only truth, that can set us free.

In the Gospel of John the religious and political establishment put Jesus to death for talking this way. In sixteenth century Christian Europe the religious and political establishment wanted to silence Luther and sought to put him to death for talking this way. He spoke the truth. It was a truth they could not stand to hear!

In that world the church had stopped telling the truth. Instead it found it much more convenient and practical to peddle the lie that Jesus wasn't really enough to get you right with God. You had to do something else. You had to do something more — like buy indulgences, obey the Pope no matter what, run off and join a monastery, make sure you went to confession or mass so many times a year, and so on.

And the flip side of that lie was another lie: You really weren't enslaved to sin. You really could do something to improve your spiritual plight if you just worked at it a little harder or followed the church's system for making it easier. Luther called it "works righteousness." In other words, sin really isn't all that bad. In fact, you can do something at least to gain a bit of God's approval. Gerhard Forde, a Lutheran theologian from Luther Seminary in the Twin Cities, spoke recently at our synod's professional worker conference. He said this about this way of thinking: "The medieval church saw God's grace as a *matching grant!*" If we are willing to contribute something, God will match our efforts with his

86

grace and mercy. In the late sixteenth century it was buying a few indulgences. What is it today?

I fear that much of what gets passed off as the gospel in the churches today is just another version of this "matching grant gospel." If you really and sincerely commit your life to Christ, then God will "match" your commitment with his grace. If you really believe, then you will be blessed. If you really tithe and give more money to the church, then God will make sure you will have enough money.

But that is not the truth. That is a lie! And the church, to be the church, needs to tell the truth. And the truth is that we are enslaved to sin and can do nothing to extricate ourselves. The truth is that the harder we try to impress God and try to win a matching grant, the more we reveal ourselves for the arrogant and self-righteous sinners that we are. Who are we to think that we can influence or manipulate God?

The only truth that can set us free from this slavery is Jesus — and only Jesus! If the church isn't telling that truth, then it is no longer the church. Then it needs to be reformed.

Such truth-telling is ultimately what sets the church apart from every other kind of organization in this world. Other clubs and associations may have rituals and holy meals and baths and their sacred books and priestly leaders. But only the church tells the truth of the gospel — the truth that can set you free!

The church is an island of truth in a sea of lies! One of the sad truths about our post-modern world is that there seems to be no one or no thing that can be counted on. Everyone is on his own to make his own way through this world. Everyone has his own agenda, his own ax to grind, his own self-interest to promote. Who can one trust in this world where the high priests are the "spin masters" who can "spin" anything to suit their own ends?

That is why truth and honesty must be so highly prized in the church. There is no substitute for telling the truth. Telling the truth is ultimately the most important thing we can offer the world.

Recently a pastor friend of mine told about an experience he had while visiting some relatives in what had been communist East Germany. One conversation he had with a young woman, who had been raised under the official atheism of the previous East German regime, was very revealing. It revealed the importance of telling the truth in a world filled with lies. She was fascinated with this pastor. He wasn't like so many other people she knew. She didn't believe in God. She distrusted religion and the state and most leaders and institutions in her cynical world. She had been betrayed and lied to so many times that she trusted no one. But she told my friend, "I trust you. You don't seem to have any ulterior motives. You are not trying to use me. You seem really to care about me."

Her reaction reveals something very important about our truth-telling in the world. The truth of our slavery to sin is so devastating, so harsh, so complete, that no one is able to face it. How can our slavery be that bad? Why should we bother to try to do anything good if God will never be impressed? Life just can't be that bad!

Yet, that is the truth! That is the truth of our slavery to sin. That is the truth that our optimistic, do-it-yourself, success-oriented culture cannot stand to hear. So, why bother to tell the truth if no one will ever listen? Because ultimately it is possible for people to face this deadly truth about themselves because of the *other truth* we have to tell. And that other truth is that contradictory truth of the gospel: in spite of our slavery to sin, God has chosen to forgive us! What we can't do for ourselves, God does for us in Jesus Christ. And we *get to* believe that!

And when we believe that truth, we are able to come to terms with the other truth. When we trust the grace and mercy of God, we are able to risk telling the truth about ourselves. We are free to admit our slavery, because God has already forgiven us.

If someone is in the hospital and has been diagnosed with terminal cancer, at first no one is going to want to face this truth. The family is going to deny it. The doctor isn't going to want to tell the patient. The patient is going to refuse to believe it. "There must be some sort of mistake! Doctor, you must have confused my diagnosis with someone else's! This can't be true! I feel fine." No one wants to tell this kind of truth. No one wants to be a bearer of news this bad. But if the patient who has been diagnosed with cancer has a good prognosis of recovery, if there is some surgery or some medicine that promises healing, it is so much easier to tell the truth. The family will be more willing to face it. The doctor will be more willing to talk about it. The patient will be more willing to accept the truth: "I have cancer!"

Because of the good news of the gospel, we can tell the bad news of our slavery to sin. Because of the truth of the gospel, we can tell the truth of sinfulness.

When something is bothering you, when some dark secret or awful sin is plaguing you, where do you go? You go to a friend to "get it off your chest." It is liberating to tell the truth to such a friend because you know that your friend can be trusted. You know that your friend will never reject you regardless of how dark your secret might be.

We *get to* tell the truth to God; we *get to* confess our sins; we *get to* come clean about the truth, because we trust the love of God, and we trust that God will never turn his back on us, no matter how awful our sin.

Notice how that gets acted out liturgically in the Brief Order of Confession and Forgivingness with which we began this service. The service began with our remembering the promise God made to us in our baptism, a promise that will never be withdrawn. As we signed ourselves with the sign of the cross and uttered those words spoken to us at our baptism, "In the name of the Father and of the Son and of the Holy Spirit," we remembered that, because of what God has done for us in Jesus Christ, we can dare to tell the truth. We can dare to admit something that the rest of the world struggles to evade and avoid at all costs. We can admit what those Jews in today's Gospel refused to admit — that we are slaves to sin and cannot save ourselves.

That confession is liberating. That confession is not something we *have to* do in order to be forgiven. On the contrary, that confession is something we *get to* do because of our faith in what God has already done for us in Jesus Christ!

Telling the truth can be a blessing to all of your life and not just your church life. Can you imagine how much better life can be if more of you would tell the truth? Because of the truth of the gospel, you can dare to tell the truth in your lives. You can live life with integrity and honesty. You don't have to make excuses or tell lies when you are wrong. You don't have to pretend to be something you are not. You don't always have to be using and manipulating others for your own gain. You don't have to be burdened by those deep dark truths that you are sure no one will understand.

You are free in Christ to tell the truth, not only about God but about yourself! In Christ you know the truth — the only truth that can make you free: the truth of what God has done and continues to do for you and the world in Jesus Christ. Yes, you are a slave to sin, but you are also the free sons and daughters of God in Jesus Christ. And that's *the truth*!

Mine Eyes Have Seen The Glory!

John 11:32-44

> *Mine eyes have seen the glory of the coming of the Lord;*
> *He is trampling out the vintage where the grapes of*
>   *wrath are stored;*
> *He has loosed the fateful lightning of his terrible swift*
>   *sword:*
> *His truth is marching on.*
> *Glory, glory! Hallelujah!*
> *Glory, glory! Hallelujah!*
> *Glory, glory! Hallelujah!*

Every time I hear these words of the "Battle Hymn of the Republic," I have visions of some old Civil War movie with soldiers marching off to meet their fate in the glory of the battlefield. In such a context this hymn takes on new meaning. Such a hymn would truly soothe any of the doubts or fears a soldier might have as he entered the bloody conflict. As the battle was about to commence, he could be sure that he was on the right side, the side of truth, of God's truth. Whether he would die or survive, simply being involved in such a holy war would assure him that he would catch a glimpse of the glory of God. That glory would come either in the victory of the battlefield or in the giving his life for a holy cause which, of course, would assure him of his place in heaven. And there in heaven he could at last see God in all of his glory.

Why did I have you sing this hymn on this All Saints' Sunday? Because on this All Saints' Sunday our thoughts turn to heaven and the eternal destiny promised to us in our baptism. We may not be about to march into battle but we surely are engaged in a kind of holy war. We are searching for a vision of glory that will inspire us to keep living and striving in a world in which our future is far from certain. Our talk about heaven is essential to the church's ability to talk of a future filled with hope. Without the hope of heaven can there be any hope for the future? How can we celebrate All Saints' Sunday without a belief in heaven?

Perhaps one of your children has perplexed you with this question. Perhaps you have asked yourself this question, unable to find a satisfactory answer. "Is there really a heaven? And if so, where is it?" Your grade schooler is having her first science class on outer space. She comes home one day, obviously deeply troubled. After some gentle probing by you, she shares with you her problem. "Dad, if astronauts travel to outer space, if we have sent people all the way to the moon, if telescopes can see billions of miles into outer space — then where is heaven?"

In Sunday school she had heard the story of Jesus' ascension, and his rising up into the skies, disappearing in the clouds, and going to heaven. She had seen artists' imaginative paintings of heaven with angels relaxing in the clouds, fluttering their wings, adjusting their halos, and playing their harps. If that heaven is "up" there, why hasn't it been discovered?

I still remember, when I was in grade school in the late 1950s at the height of the Cold War between the U. S. and Russia, how Russian cosmonaut Yuri Gagarin, the first man in space, had triumphantly announced to the world that he had been "up there" and he had seen neither God nor heaven. Of course, his comments pleased the leaders of the communist government and supported their official atheism.

The question of heaven (Where is it?) is a timely one for us to consider on this All Saints' Sunday. This is that one day during the church year when we make a special effort to remember and celebrate all of those saints of faith who have been this way before us and are now departed. We remember such saints as Abraham, Moses, Isaiah, Mary, the mother of our Lord, Peter, Paul, Martin Luther, Martin Luther King, Jr., and so on. We look to the example of their lives for inspiration as we struggle with what it means to live the Christian life.

A day to remember the saints of the church has had a long history. In the third century the church set aside a special day to remember those who had been martyred, who sacrificed their lives for the faith. It was not, however, until the eighth century in the Celtic lands of Great Britain that November 1 became associated with a day to commemorate the saints. In that part of the world, this day seemed to be natural for this sort of thing. This was a time of the year when the late autumn frost thickly blanketed the ground with an eerie white cover and suggested to many that the spirits of the dead had made a visit. From this Christian holiday came our modern secularized holiday called "All Saints Eve" or "All Hallows Eve" or "Halloween."

Last month we buried Esther Hilker, a long-time member of this congregation. Many of us mourned Esther's passing. I am sure that her grandchildren wondered about their grandmother's fate. Where is Grandma now? Is she merely buried in her tomb, slowly returning to dust and ashes? At Esther's funeral we sang and spoke of her now being in heaven. But, again, where is that heaven? Is it "up," "down," "beyond"?

The church along with Holy Scripture has described heaven as the abode of God. Heaven is where God is. But where is God? And isn't God supposed to be everywhere in creation? Then where is heaven? Everywhere? Nowhere? Somewhere? It is so difficult to speak of a dimension of existence which is very different from life as we know it. Yet, to deny the existence of heaven would make our Christian faith and hope for the future empty and meaningless.

Such questions about the nature of heaven are more than just expressions of our curiosity. They are reflections of a much deeper anxiety, something that touches each of us in a very personal way. Such questions take on a special sense of urgency not only because we are concerned about the destiny of our departed loved ones (Has God abandoned them? Are they in misery or ecstasy or somewhere in between? Do they have a future?), but also because we are anxious about our own destiny. What does the future hold? What about us? What lies beyond death for you and me? Is this

93

life all there is? Or is there more? And if there is, is it heaven or hell or somewhere in between?

Maybe what we need to do is to stop thinking of heaven as a place somewhere "up there," above, in the sky. When we confess in the Apostles' Creed that Jesus "ascended into heaven and is seated at the right hand of the Father," we don't literally mean that there is a specific place in heaven where Jesus is sitting or that God actually has a right hand, a left hand, a right foot, a left foot, and so on. What we are really saying is that Jesus has been honored by his Father for the job he performed faithfully on earth. "At the right hand" means a place of privilege and honor. With apologies to any left-handed people here this morning, as a right-handed person uses his right hand to do what he does best, so also, when God is doing what he really wants to do in this world, when God is doing that for which he wants to be best known, he does it through the risen and ascended Jesus "at his right hand." Jesus is God's "right-hand man," so to speak.

So, where is heaven? It is wherever Jesus is present acting as God's right-hand man. And where is that? Jesus is present doing his heavenly thing wherever the forgiveness of sins is being offered. Martin Luther once said, "Where there is forgiveness of sins, there is also life and salvation." In other words, heaven is where Jesus is present doing God's right-handed thing, i.e., forgiving sinners.

Where is heaven? Heaven is where the waters of Baptism are poured and the name of God is spoken. Heaven is where the body and blood of Jesus are offered in bread and wine. Heaven is where the guilty are released from their deadly past through the granting of forgiveness. Heaven is where the stranglehold of death and hopelessness is broken: when enemies embrace, when spouses reconcile, when neighbors are neighborly, when victims refuse to get even, when the powerful offer to serve instead of demanding that they be served.

When we sing, "Mine eyes have seen the coming of the glory of the Lord," we are not just singing of some glory we have yet to see, some glory that lies somewhere indefinitely in the future. No, we are making the outrageous claim that we have *already* seen the glory of the Lord! We have already caught a glimpse of heaven! We have already seen that place where death has been defeated, where there are no more tears, where there is only joy and celebration.

We have seen Jesus. We have seen Jesus in the ministry of this congregation, in the lives of its members, and in the Word proclaimed in our midst, the breaking of bread, and the pouring of water.

In today's Gospel we saw this Jesus raise from the dead his friend, Lazarus of Bethany. Lazarus had been dead four days before Jesus finally arrived. Lazarus' sisters, Mary and Martha, were disappointed that Jesus had not come sooner. Perhaps if Jesus had been there before Lazarus died, he might have been able to do something. But now it is too late. Lazarus is long dead, four days dead, so dead that his body has begun to decay in the tomb. But Jesus will not be thwarted. He is determined to display the glory of God. He is determined to give those people gathered there at the tomb of Lazarus outside of Bethany a glimpse of the glory of God. And he does it. He raises Lazarus from the dead.

That's fine. Once upon a time in a faraway place Jesus raised someone by the name of Lazarus from the dead. Jesus displayed the glory of God. I am sure all of those people were impressed. They got their beloved friend back from the dead. They knew they were in the presence of someone special. He was heavenly. He was "out of this world." He had power over death. If they had known the song, I am sure they would have broken into a chorus of "Mine eyes have seen the glory of the coming of the Lord."

That's fine, but so what? What did those people think when Lazarus died again, which he surely did? Lazarus didn't live forever. What did they think when they saw their friends and loved ones die? What did they think when they came face to face with their own mortality?

And what about us? I haven't seen anyone raised from the dead lately, especially someone who has been dead for four days. I still see people dropping off like flies. The death rate is still 100 percent.

All of this talk of heaven seems rather farfetched, doesn't it? Why should anyone believe all this stuff? We are making some fairly outrageous claims when we claim that this community is a bit of heaven on earth. Thunder doesn't rumble and lightning doesn't flash when someone is baptized. The bread and wine of communion doesn't seem to taste like body and blood. This communion of saints still behaves an awful lot like sinners. And what right do we have to forgive the most outrageous of sins — and do it in the name of God? And what about heaven? In this world of broken dreams and broken lives and broken promises, how can we dare to speak of heaven — especially heaven here, among us, now?

Every year when I meet with the confirmation students I try to help them come to grips with this problem. When they complete their confirmation instruction and they come forward to confess their faith before the congregation, they are doing an outrageous thing. In a sense they are saying, "Mine eyes have seen the glory of coming of the Lord...."

I ask them if anyone knows what a saint is. There is usually silence. So, I give them a definition. A saint is someone who is special. A saint is someone whom God has chosen. A saint is someone whom God has set aside. A saint is someone perfect, sinless. A saint is not just dead in the ground. A saint is in heaven.

Then, I ask them the big question: Does anyone think he or she is a saint?

The class is silent for a few moments until one or two courageous souls hesitantly raise their hands. Then I quiz them. Do they really think they are saints? Do they really think they are perfect? I bet if I asked their brother or sister or parents, they would give me plenty of evidence to prove that they are not even close to being saints. They are a lot more like hell on earth than heaven on earth.

The few courageous souls drop their hands. They aren't so sure any more.

I ask them again. "Whoever thinks you are a saint, raise your hand."

Aha! They now know what answer the pastor is looking for. The right answer is "No." No one is a saint. So, no one raises a hand the second time I ask the question. They know better now. They have learned their lesson well.

Then it is time for the punch line. Then is it time for the surprise. Then it is time to make the outrageous announcement. Then it is time to let them experience how incredible this Christian faith is. Then it is time to proclaim the gospel!

"All of you — raise your hands."

And they all stare at one another in disbelief. What is the pastor doing? Has he gone off the deep end? This doesn't make any sense.

"Yes, this doesn't make any sense, but this is the startling truth: You are all saints! You are perfect, sinless, the apple of God's eye. You are already in heaven — not because you are better than anyone else, not because you have not committed any sins, not because you have kept all the commandments. No, you are saints *because God says so!* You are saints because you are baptized. You are saints because Jesus suffered, died, and was raised again for you! You are saints because you have seen the glory of God!"

I remind them that everything during their time of confirmation study will be about getting them to believe that outrageous promise and to discover the implications of that belief for their lives.

But, so what? Why should they believe me? Why should they believe that this is true? Why should they believe that there is heaven not only beyond the grave, but, even more incredibly, here and now?

Because I believe it. And I believe it because others before me have believed it. And they believed it because thousands before them believed it. They staked their lives on it. Many of them gave their lives for it. There is no other way to explain why so many for so long have believed something so incredible. It must be true.

People, we believe because the church believes. Were it not for all those saints who have gone before us, we would not believe. Were it not for those believers, who not only saw Jesus raise Lazarus from the dead that day long ago outside of Bethany but also saw that same Jesus raised from the dead on Easter, we would not believe. An outrageous announcement like the gospel is not something people make up and then sacrifice their lives for it.

Were it not for those saints who have gone before us, we could not see the glory. We could not be touched by heaven. We could not believe the gospel. We could not know that we too are saints. We could not join that holy band that has gone before us in singing, "Mine eyes have seen the glory of the coming of the Lord...." *(Motion the congregation to rise and join in singing.)*

No Freudian Slip!

Matthew 6:25-33

It's late afternoon but it is still several hours before supper is served. You are hungry. You remember that cookie jar in the kitchen and decide to indulge yourself in a little afternoon snack. You open the jar already imagining the taste of those chocolate chip cookies. But the cookie jar is empty! No cookies! Who ate them? You turn around, and standing there behind you, looking up at you with a funny look on his face, is your six-year-old. "I didn't do it, Daddy. I didn't eat those last four chocolate chip cookies!" How did he know about those last four cookies in the jar? And you know you are staring at the culprit. A slip of the tongue betrayed the villain and revealed the truth.

Some twenty years ago my wife and I spent a summer studying and traveling in Germany. We had only been in the country a few days when we discovered "the ugly American." Repeatedly we ran into large tour groups of Americans who were often rude and obnoxious. They seemed to think that yelling at the Germans would somehow make their English more understandable. We decided that we did not want to be associated with such boors. So, whenever the ugly American tourists would approach us to ask for help, we would pretend to be German and not able to understand them. "Ich verstehe nicht." But occasionally our deception would fail. An English word would slip from our lips, and we would betray our identity. Inadvertently we had revealed a truth we had wanted to keep hidden.

In our popular vernacular such slips of the tongue are called "Freudian slips." The great Austrian thinker and father of psychotherapy, Sigmund Freud, is known for discovering that buried deep within the subconscious of every one of us are thoughts, desires, and urges of which we are usually unaware. But the sub-conscious does affect our behavior. Occasionally these subconscious thoughts will reveal themselves through our behavior, perhaps through our "slips of the tongue." Such Freudian slips betray our true inner feelings, feelings which we may have wanted to avoid, feelings of which we may have been totally unaware.

At the center of today's Gospel is such a Fredudian slip: worry. Most of us assume that it is just a natural part of life, part of being human. We assure ourselves that a certain amount of worry about tomorrow is even healthy. It motivates us to work and plan for the future. Of course, too much worry can create problems. Yes, always worrying about the future, about what to wear or what to eat, can become an unhealthy obsession. We are opposed to that kind of worry.

But where do you draw the line? When does a healthy concern for the future become a self-destructive obsession about tomorrow?

Jesus is uninterested in such distinctions. He offers no helpful guidelines. Instead, Jesus sees such worry as a Freudian slip, a revelation of something much deeper and more dangerous within us. Even the most simple of worries exposes something which we all want to avoid. It exposes something of which we may not even be aware. It exposes something which we may be too embarrassed to admit: our lack of faith in God.

The lectionary editors who chose this passage from Jesus' Sermon on the Mount decided to leave out verse 24. I think that was a big mistake. Verse 24 sets the context for Jesus' comments on worry. In verse 24 Jesus makes a claim about what is really going on in our hearts and minds when we worry about what we will eat or what we will wear.

"No one can serve two masters; for a slave will either hate the one and love the other, or be devoted to the one and despise the other. You cannot serve God and wealth."

What we assume are our innocent and everyday worries are, in fact, Freudian slips. They reveal what is really going on within us. They expose the fact that we are breaking the first commandment. We are not trusting God. We are serving another master. We are idolaters.

106

This seems too harsh a judgment on the part of Jesus. He seems to be jumping to an unwarranted conclusion. Since when is worrying about what I will wear to work or what I will cook for supper a sign of my unfaith?

Martin Luther's comments on the first commandment in the *Large Catechism* are helpful here. Luther points our how all of us have our gods. Humans are incurably theolatrous. We all have those gods, those things, which give our lives meaning and purpose. Look at what excites us and motivates us, and that is our god. Look at what we worry about, what makes us anxious, what we fear losing, and that is our god. Like Jesus before him, Luther is making a profoundly devastating observation about the human condition. We all have dirty hands. None of us is clean. We are all guilty. We all sin. We all break the first commandment every day. We all serve another master.

Jesus must have known that his disciples were worriers just like us. So when he tells them not to worry, he is really accusing them. "Look at the birds of the air ... Consider the lilies of the field ...." They don't worry. They don't scurry about trying to buy the latest fashions at the year's best sale. They don't have their days rise and fall on the basis of the latest Dow Jones average. They don't count calories and grams of fat in order to be sure they keep that svelte figure and attract the admiring glances of the opposite sex. So why do we do these things, we who are worth so much more in the eyes of God? Why do we worry? Jesus makes the embarrassing accusation in verse 30. We have "little faith." We don't trust God. We break the first commandment. We are serving another master.

Our worry, even the simplest of worries, is a Freudian slip. It reveals the secret we want to keep hidden not only from God but also from ourselves: we are people of little faith.

Instead of worrying about tomorrow, we ought to trust God. We ought to be thankful. I suspect that this is why this passage was chosen for this Thanksgiving Day. Jesus directs our attention to the wonders of nature — the birds of the air and the lilies of the field. And how about all the wonderful and bountiful things that fill the world around you? And how about the affluence that you people in this community enjoy? You are blessed! So, why aren't you thankful? Why are you worrying about tomorrow, you people of little faith?

Jesus is shaming us into a sense of thanksgiving. But such thanksgiving is easier said than done. Despite our best intentions, our giving thanks is always less than what it should be. And there are always the Freudian slips that reveal that this is precisely the case.

Recently I had an experience that was a revealing Freudian slip. I was in the midst of making a presentation to the junior high youth gathered for our Sunday night youth program when one of the young people took me aside and told me that there was someone here to see me. Who could this be? I would never have scheduled an appointment with anyone during these important Sunday night sessions with the youth.

I went to the back of the room and there stood a nervous, somewhat shabbily dressed black male. He said he had to talk to the pastor, to me, right then. And it had to be in private. I led him into my office and offered him a seat. I must admit I had some anxiety wondering what was so important that this fellow had to see me immediately and in private. It was then that Ronald Reed told me a most extraordinary story.

He was apologetic and self-conscious. He had just been discharged from St. Vincent's Hospital. He had been a patient there, receiving dialysis courtesy of government welfare. He pulled out his discharge papers and showed me that his story was true. He then rolled up his shirt sleeves and showed me his forearms, both grossly misshapen and discolored, skin bulging with huge lumps, the results of his frequent encounters with dialysis. I suspected that this was not your typical street swindler on the make for another victim. I felt that his story was true. At least I wanted to believe that it was true.

He said he was desperate and had no place to go. He had called a local church and found out that there was a large community service going on that night in town, but he didn't know where it was. So he asked for a ride with someone from the hospital to the downtown. Our church had lots of cars in the parking lot, and he thought this might be the place of the service and where he might get some help.

He was right. There was such a service going on that night, but it was not at this church. It was the community Thanksgiving service, and it was going to start in about fifteen minutes at another church, and I was on my way. In fact, I was going to be one of the participating clergy. I didn't have much money, but I was moved by his story and his sincerity. I gave him two twenty-dollar bills that I had in my wallet. I invited him to ride with me over to the Episcopal church where the service would shortly be starting.

On the way over Ronald Reed told me how scared he was to be in town. There weren't any black people out here in this distant suburb, so he feared for his safety. I silently chuckled, knowing that most of the people out here would be more afraid of him than he was of them. His fears were unfounded. However, I suspect that the local police would regard such a rare black with suspicion. They may not have been so hospitable. When we arrived at the church, the parking lot was almost full. We had to park a distance from the entrance. During our walk across the parking lot, Ronald was nervous and silent. The closer we got to the entrance, the more he distanced himself from me. He thanked me for the ride and the help and said he would see me inside.

I was running so late that I forgot all about Ronald until I entered the sanctuary in the clergy procession and saw him standing alone in one of the rear pews. He was trying to sing this grand and glorious thanksgiving hymn that I am sure was not part of the African-American musical tradition. He stuck out like a sore thumb in this beautiful house of worship, not only because of his blackness but also because of his shabby dress and his isolation. No one sat within five pews of him, as if he was some kind of leper.

The service was magnificent. There were choirs from several different churches creating beautiful music. There were the sounds of a magnificent pipe organ. There was a fine sermon reminding us of how we needed to be thankful for the great bounty with which God has blessed us. The well-dressed congregation was vivid evidence of why we needed to be there giving thanks.

But then I saw the dark face of Ronald Reed in the back and wondered what he thought about all this talk of God's bountiful blessings and our need to be thankful. I thought of his shabby clothes, his bulging arms disfigured from many rounds of dialysis, his fear of the whites in town, his quiet despair. In my mind his presence challenged the credibility of everything we were doing in that service. How can we thank God when there are so many with so little in this world? What kind of God is it who would permit such gross disparity between the haves and the have-nots? How can we be praising God for such bountiful blessings when there, sitting in the back of the sanctuary for everyone to see, is someone who obviously has not been so blessed? This whole service finally seemed grotesque, dishonest, a self-righteous exercise in self-congratulation.

When the grand and glorious procession marched out of the sanctuary at the close of the service, I saw something very odd, very strange, very revealing. It was a Freudian slip of massive proportions. As the congregation left the sanctuary and mingled in the narthex, Ronald Reed was totally ignored. No one said a word to him. He was avoided like the plague. No one wanted to acknowledge his presence.

Why? Were they afraid of him? I don't think anyone had to fear for their safety, but they, we, all of us, were afraid of him. Why? Because his presence challenged the credibility of our service. His presence reminded us that all is not well with this world, that there are gross inequities, that there are many who are not blessed with such bounty. And such reminders scare us. We all silently fear that "there but for the grace of God go I." Isn't that why many of us live out in the suburbs — to be safe, not to have to worry about the dangers of being around people who are different and who have less than we do and who may be carefully planning some way to get some of that stuff away from us?

Did God send us Ronald Reed that night? I don't know. But I do know one thing. Our avoidance of someone like Ronald Reed was very revealing. It was a Fredudian slip. It exposed the fear and worry still lurking in the hearts of all of us, despite our songs of praise and thanksgiving which had sounded just moments before. Keeping our distance from the one whose presence contradicted the whole thrust of this Thanksgiving service revealed that we were still anxious, worried, afraid of losing our bounty.

We had just sung our lungs out praising God! Didn't we say that we trusted and believed in him? But this Freudian slip revealed a crack in the armor. We still were anxious about tomorrow. We still had doubts about God's benevolence. And so we had to avoid Ronald Reed. He exposed our little faith.

The truth is that our lives are filled with Freudian slips revealing our little faith. We nervously watch the daily gyrations of the stock market. We hang on every word spoken by Federal Reserve Chairman Alan Greenspan. We live and die for a bargain. We panic about the future of Social Security.

But look at the birds of the air, the lilies of the field, the grass, which is full and lush in the morning but limp and wilted after a day in the hot sun, ready to be thrown into the fiery oven. Could this be the fate of those like us who have such little faith? Could those who fail to trust in God end up in the burning oven? Jesus seems to be hinting as much.

In the face of such a deadly fate, Jesus offers us another alternative. And Jesus is clear and unequivocal. There is no Freudian slip here. Jesus offers himself. When he invites his disciples to seek first the kingdom of God and its righteousness, he is referring to himself. Jesus embodied the kingdom. Jesus was the manifestation of God's rule in this world. And as Jesus welcomed sinners and doubters and outcasts and tax collectors and whores and all of those who seemed to be miserable failures when it came to trusting God, he was sending a message to his worried and anxious disciples who always seemed to be fretting about what they would eat or what they should wear. God still forgives them. God still embraces them even with their little faith. God can be trusted — even when everything else in life is uncertain and fraught with risk.

Yes, God can still be trusted, no matter what. And if God can be trusted, then what is there to worry about? Why bother to wring your hands and be anxious about tomorrow? Tomorrow is in the gracious hands of God.

Lectionary Preaching After Pentecost

Virtually all pastors who make use of the sermons in this book will find their worship life and planning shaped by one of two lectionary series. Most mainline Protestant denominations, along with clergy of the Roman Catholic Church, have now approved — either for provisional or official use — the three-year Revised Common (Consensus) Lectionary. This family of denominations includes United Methodist, Presbyterian, United Church of Christ and Disciples of Christ. Recently the ELCA division of Lutheranism also began following the Revised Common Lectionary. This change has been reflected in the headings and scripture listings with each sermon in this book.

Roman Catholics and Lutheran divisions other than ELCA follow their own three-year cycle of texts. While there are divergences between the Revised Common and Roman Catholic/Lutheran systems, the gospel texts show striking parallels, with few text selections evidencing significant differences. Nearly all the gospel texts included in this book will, therefore, be applicable to worship and preaching planning for clergy following either lectionary.

A significant divergence does occur, however, in the method by which specific gospel texts are assigned to specific calendar days. The Revised Common and Roman Catholic Lectionaries accomplish this by counting backwards from Christ the King (Last Sunday after Pentecost), discarding "extra" texts from the front of the list: Lutherans (not using the Revised Common Lectionary) follow the opposite pattern, counting forward from The Holy Trinity, discarding "extra" texts at the end of the list.

The following index will aid the user of this book in matching the correct text to the correct Sunday during the Pentecost portion of the church year.

(Fixed dates do not pertain to Lutheran Lectionary)

Fixed Date Lectionaries *Revised Common (including ELCA)* *and Roman Catholic*	**Lutheran Lectionary** *Lutheran*
The Day of Pentecost	The Day of Pentecost
The Holy Trinity	The Holy Trinity
May 29-June 4 — Proper 4, Ordinary Time 9	Pentecost 2
June 5-11 — Proper 5, Ordinary Time 10	Pentecost 3
June 12-18 — Proper 6, Ordinary Time 11	Pentecost 4
June 19-25 — Proper 7, Ordinary Time 12	Pentecost 5

113

June 26-July 2 — Proper 8, Ordinary Time 13	Pentecost 6
July 3-9 — Proper 9, Ordinary Time 14	Pentecost 7
July 10-16 — Proper 10, Ordinary Time 15	Pentecost 8
July 17-23 — Proper 11, Ordinary Time 16	Pentecost 9
July 24-30 — Proper 12, Ordinary Time 17	Pentecost 10
July 31-Aug. 6 — Proper 13, Ordinary Time 18	Pentecost 11
Aug. 7-13 — Proper 14, Ordinary Time 19	Pentecost 12
Aug. 14-20 — Proper 15, Ordinary Time 20	Pentecost 13
Aug. 21-27 — Proper 16, Ordinary Time 21	Pentecost 14
Aug. 28-Sept. 3 — Proper 17, Ordinary Time 22	Pentecost 15
Sept. 4-10 — Proper 18, Ordinary Time 23	Pentecost 16
Sept. 11-17 — Proper 19, Ordinary Time 24	Pentecost 17
Sept. 18-24 — Proper 20, Ordinary Time 25	Pentecost 18
Sept. 25-Oct. 1 — Proper 21, Ordinary Time 26	Pentecost 19
Oct. 2-8 — Proper 22, Ordinary Time 27	Pentecost 20
Oct. 9-15 — Proper 23, Ordinary Time 28	Pentecost 21
Oct. 16-22 — Proper 24, Ordinary Time 29	Pentecost 22
Oct. 23-29 — Proper 25, Ordinary Time 30	Pentecost 23
Oct. 30-Nov. 5 — Proper 26, Ordinary Time 31	Pentecost 24
Nov. 6-12 — Proper 27, Ordinary Time 32	Pentecost 25
Nov. 13-19 — Proper 28, Ordinary Time 33	Pentecost 26
	Pentecost 27
Nov. 20-26 — Christ the King	Christ the King

Reformation Day (or last Sunday in October) is October 31 (Revised Common, Lutheran)

All Saints' Day (or first Sunday in November) is November 1 (Revised Common, Lutheran, Roman Catholic)

Books In This Cycle B Series

GOSPEL SET
A God For This World
Sermons for Advent/Christmas/Epiphany
Maurice A. Fetty

The Culture Of Disbelief
Sermons For Lent/Easter
Donna E. Schaper

The Advocate
Sermons For Sundays After Pentecost (First Third)
Ron Lavin

Surviving In A Cordless World
Sermons For Sundays After Pentecost (Middle Third)
Lawrence H. Craig

Against The Grain — Words For A Politically Incorrect Church
Sermons For Sundays After Pentecost (Last Third)
Steven E. Albertin

FIRST LESSON SET
Defining Moments
Sermons For Advent/Christmas/Epiphany
William L. Self

From This Day Forward
Sermons For Lent/Easter
Paul W. Kummer

Out From The Ordinary
Sermons For Sundays After Pentecost (First Third)
Gary L. Carver

Wearing The Wind
Sermons For Sundays After Pentecost (Middle Third)
Stephen M. Crotts

Out Of The Whirlwind
Sermons For Sundays After Pentecost (Last Third)
John A. Stroman

SECOND LESSON SET
Humming Till The Music Returns
Sermons For Advent/Christmas/Epiphany
Wayne Brouwer

Ashes To Ascension
Sermons For Lent/Easter
John A. Stroman